The London Coffee Guide.
2011

Edited by
Jeffrey Young
and Christine Shanahan

Author: Allegra Strategies
Photography: Warattaya S. Bullôt
& Christine Shanahan
Design: John Osborne
Website: Tim Spring
Publisher: Allegra Strategies Ltd

Allegra
STRATEGIES

Published in 2010 by Allegra Strategies Ltd No.1 Northumberland Ave, Trafalgar Square, London, WC2N 5BW

Visit our website:
www.londoncoffeeguide.com

All information was accurate at time of going to press.

Published by *Allegra* STRATEGIES Ltd © 2010
No.1 Northumberland Ave, Trafalgar Square, London, WC2N 5BW

Foreword

London's coffee culture has changed dramatically over the last two years.

London's cafés and roasters are internationally known - we have world champions, coffee tourists, baristas coming to London to learn their craft and we no longer have to listen to the "there is no good coffee in London" phrase anymore.

The explosion of good coffee did not come out of nowhere. It has been a long journey, likened to wading through treacle. I joined London's journey in 1998 in search of a café scene I had been part of in NZ. All I found was bitter ashy frustration, few people knew what I was talking about and the UK was heading for a love affair with a 16oz skinny dry hazelnut cappuccino.

I spent London's wilderness years at Monmouth Coffee, deservedly an institution that kept the flame alive. Here I learnt about farms, varietals, processing methods and customer service. The first sign of change in the London coffee scene came from the arrival of a café called Flat White on Berwick St. After a brief period of adjustment the wave of cafés came thick and fast, each building on what the previous had done.

Being part of building the foundation for quality cafés and roasters to flourish in London has been disheartening at times but ultimately satisfying. After years of working in the barista wilderness this development of London coffee has me fearing complacency. Yes we have come a long way, but we cannot honestly believe we are giving the best coffee, service and experience possible. Coffee is still in its infancy and the journey will be great fun, so let's keep pushing, exploring and enjoying.

Gwilym Davies
2009 UK AND WORLD BARISTA CHAMPION

Contents

Introduction

Welcome to The London Coffee Guide 2011 - The definitive guide to London's Top 100 coffee venues.

The London Coffee Guide was born out of a constant quest to find great places to go for coffee in London. These places used to be few and far between in the capital, however London is now home to a thriving independent coffee scene and both locals and visitors are spoilt for choice.

We have created this guide to assist and inform people who are willing to travel across this wonderful city in the hunt for great coffee venues.

It might be the coffee itself that is the main attraction, or perhaps the excitement of visiting a new and unique coffee shop. Our aim is to encourage fellow coffee lovers to try something different and discover places they otherwise may never have known existed.

Allegra Strategies is a well-established leader in research and business intelligence to the coffee industry in the UK and Europe. We have drawn on this research as well as countless other sources (including industry experts, blogs, general community views and staff of the coffee venues themselves) to bring you The London Coffee Guide.

About the Guide

Ratings

Every venue that appears in The London Coffee Guide has been visited and rated by our expert team. The ratings fall into two distinct categories: **Coffee Rating** and **Overall Rating**.

Coffee Rating

The coffee rating is not only about the taste of the coffee. It also takes into account numerous other 'coffee credentials' such as the coffee roaster, equipment used, barista skills, visual appeal of the coffee and several other factors that demonstrate the venue's overall attitude to coffee.

The following question is the guiding principle used to determine the coffee ratings: **To what extent does this coffee venue deliver an amazing coffee experience?**

Overall Rating

In combination with the coffee experience the overall rating considers to what extent the coffee shop experience delivers a 'wow factor' to the customer. Elements that are taken into account include store environment, ambience, design, customer service and food quality among other factors.

To determine a coffee shop's overall rating the following question is used as the guiding principle: **How do the combination of coffee and the coffee shop experience translate to exceptional levels of customer excitement?**

The London Coffee Guide includes coffee carts, stalls and kiosks as well as coffee shops. It was not considered fair to compare these venues with permanent venues in terms of overall experience and therefore coffee stalls, carts and kiosks have only been given a coffee rating.

Symbols used throughout The London Coffee Guide:

 Coffee beans sold on site

 Decaf available

 Gluten free products available

 Venue has a loyalty card

 Venue part of 'disloyalty card' across various coffee shops

 Soya milk available

 Toilets

 Mother & baby friendly

 Disabled access

 WiFi available

 Alcohol license

Allegra Foundation is an independent registered charity (No. 1133540) **founded by Allegra Strategies Limited**.

The Foundation manages the charitable initiative **Project Waterfall**, which endeavours to provide clean drinking water to impoverished communities in coffee producing countries in Africa. In many parts of the world, and frequently in coffee producing countries, a lack of access to clean drinking water is causing severe hardship to millions of people. The first project will be funded in 2011 and delivered in partnership with WaterAid to provide clean drinking water to 7,000 people in the Chini Ward of the Mbulu District, Tanzania.

20% of all profits from The London Coffee Guide 2011 will go to Project Waterfall.

A Brief History of London Coffee Shops

The Early Years

800 AD The coffee plant (Coffea) attracts human interest and consumption as early as 800 AD in the Kaffe region of Ethiopia. According to legend, it was an Ethiopian goat herder named Kaldi who first discovered how animated his herd of goats became after chewing on the red berries.

Mid 17th Century

Travellers to Middle Eastern countries introduce coffee as a new beverage in Britain.

1650 The first English coffee house is established in Oxford in 1650 by a Jewish man named Jacob at the Angel in the parish of St Peter.

Coffee houses become meeting places for political and literary debates between artists, intellectuals, merchants and bankers. Such venues are known as Penny Universities, in reference to the one penny entrance fee. They are closely associated with reading and provide pamphlets and newspapers as well as copious amounts of coffee.

1652 London's first coffee house is established by Pasqua Rosée in St Michael's Alley, Cornhill, London EC3.

1668 Edward Lloyd's Coffee House in Lombard Street becomes a key meeting place for ship owners and marine insurance brokers. Situated where Lloyd's headquarters are located today, this must be considered a major factor behind London becoming the modern world hub for insurance and financial services.

1674 The Women's Petition Against Coffee is set up in London in response to men's lack of time spent at home from the 'excessive use of the drying and enfeebling liquor'.

1675 There are now more than 3,000 coffee houses across England. King Charles II attempts to outlaw the use of coffee houses because he regards them as hotbeds of revolution, but following large public protests his proclamation is revoked after 11 days.

1680 Jonathan's Coffee House is established by Jonathan Miles in Change Alley. It is a place where stockbrokers frequently meet and eventually becomes today's London Stock Exchange.

1706 Thomas Twining opens the first known tea room which remains at 216 Strand today.

18th Century

Coffee houses gradually decline in popularity when they start charging more than one penny for entrance. They therefore became elite establishments, while travelling taverns became more popular social spaces. Coffee also becomes a less important commodity as the East India Trade Company and British trade focus more on tea imports from East India.

Last Century

1894 Lyons opens a chain of tea rooms, followed by Lyons Corner Houses in London's West End in 1906.

1923 The Kenya Coffee Company Limited (Kenco) is established and soon begins selling coffee on Vere Street Mayfair.

1950s Formica table topped, Italian-run Espresso Houses are a popular feature of this era, particulary in London's Soho area.

1952 Moka Bar opens in Frith Street as London's first Espresso Bar.

1971 Starbucks opens first store at Pike

Place Market in Seattle, USA.

First Costa Coffee shop opened by brothers Sergio and Bruno Costa at 9 Newport Street, London.

1978 An early pioneer of artisan coffee, Monmouth Coffee Company opens in Monmouth Street, Covent Garden.

1986 Pret A Manger established by college friends Julian Metcalf and Sinclair Beecham.

1992 Fairtrade Foundation is established in London by CAFOD, Christian Aid, Oxfam, Traidcraft and the World Development Movement and is soon followed by the Women's Institute.

1995 Whitbread Group acquires Costa Coffee with 41 stores and a roastery in Lambeth.

1997 Nescafé opens first Café Nescafé trial stores in London and UK but closes all outlets several years later.

Gerry Ford acquires 5 Caffè Nero stores and begins building a chain which grows to become the third largest coffee shop brand in the UK.

1998 Starbucks launches in the UK, acquiring 65 Seattle Coffee Company stores for an estimated £52 million.

1999 Allegra Strategies releases ground-breaking Project Café Report predicting a significant boom in coffee shops.

Last Decade

2000 Internet cafés grow in popularity during the dotcom era.

Marks & Spencer launches Café Revive concept.

2001 Caffé Latte beverage is added to the Consumer Price Index (CPI), the basket of goods which the government uses to measure products purchased by a typical British household.

2006 The number of branded chain coffee shop outlets exceeds 1,000 in London alone.

2007 Flat White coffee shop opens in Berwick Street, Soho setting the stage for further antipodean influences.

James Hoffman crowned World Barista Champion and founds Square Mile Coffee.

McDonald's sells stake in Pret A Manger to Bridgepoint Capital and Goldman Sachs, valuing the business at £351 million.

2008 First ever European Coffee Symposium held at London's Park Lane Hotel.

2009 A host of new artisan 'third wave' coffee shops open in London.

UK's Gwilym Davies crowned World Barista Champion.

2010 Growth of artisan coffee shops and micro coffee roasteries in London continues to accelerate.

Costa, Starbucks and several other mainstream coffee chains launch antipodean beverage 'flat white'.

World Barista Championships held in London at Caffè Culture.

McDonald's UK launches espresso coffees.

Arrival of NZ-based Allpress Espresso Roastery in Redchurch Street Shoreditch.

Launch of first-ever London Coffee Guide.

" Hand-crafted, credible coffee. "

Grand Cru Coffee
Chosen for its unique character, complexity and extraordinary, rich flavour, Grand Cru is a fully traceable coffee - sourced from some of the finest coffee plantations around the globe.

For more information, or to find out where you can taste our fantastic Grand Cru coffee, contact United Coffee UK on **01908 275 555** or visit

www.unitedcoffeeuk.com

GrandCrü
credible coffee.

u unitedcoffee

GrandCrü
credible coffee.

West End

London's West End is renowned for its famous theatres, fashion stores and nightlife. The area's vibrant coffee scene is continually moving forward, driven by new concepts and showbiz flair.

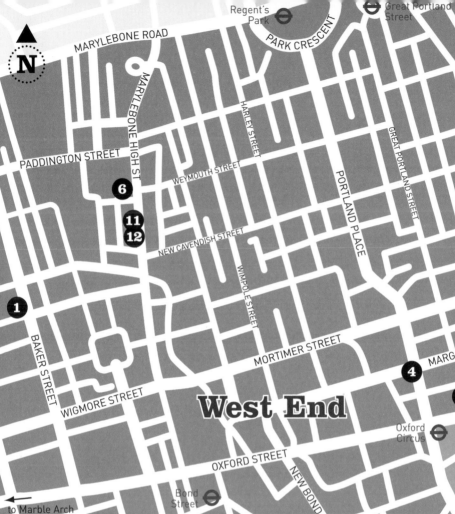

COFFEE VENUES KEY.

West End

1 **Apostrophe** Baker Street
2 **Caffè Nero** Bedford Street
3 **Costa Coffee** Great Portland Street
4 **Joe And The Juice** Regent Street
5 **Kaffeine**
6 **La Fromagerie** Marylebone
7 **Lantana**
8 **Monmouth Coffee Company** Covent Garden
9 **Napket** Piccadilly
10 **Notes, Music and Coffee**
11 **Patisserie Valerie** Marylebone
12 **The Providores**
13 **Reynolds** Charlotte Street
14 **Starbucks** Conduit Street
15 **Tapped & Packed**

Soho

16 **Bar Italia**
17 **Brewed Boy Espresso**
18 **Fernandez & Wells Café**
19 **Fernandez & Wells Espresso Bar**
20 **Flat White**
21 **Foxcroft & Ginger**
22 **Joe & The Juice** Broadwick Street
23 **LJ Coffee House**
24 **Milkbar**
25 **Princi**
26 **Sacred** Ganton Street

Apostrophe Baker Street
19 Baker Street, W1U 8EQ

This Apostrophe is modern and inviting, appealing to both shopping-weary tourists and local business workers on a quick lunch break. Apostrophe's signature black and magenta dominate the room, but a luminous feature wall at the rear combines with large side windows to create a light-filled and open environment to enjoy a coffee.

Sister coffee shops.
15 other locations in London

Images supplied by Apostrophe

OPEN.

Mon-Fri.	7:15am - 6:00pm
Sat.	8:30am - 6:00pm
Sun.	9:00am - 5:30pm

OVERVIEW.

Catergory
Eatery
Owner
Amir Chen
First opened
2008

COFFEE & EQUIPMENT.

Coffee roaster
Darlington's
Coffee machine
La Cimbali M32 Dosatron DT4,
2 groups
Coffee grinder
Mazzer Super Jolly

COFFEE PRICING.

Espresso	£1.40 / £1.60
Cappucino	£2.00 / £2.35 / £2.65
Latte	£2.00 / £2.35 / £2.65
Flat white	£2.00 / £2.35

FOOD.

Gourmet sandwiches, salads, fresh
pastries and baked sweet treats are
nicely presented on the counter

CONTACT.

+44(0)20 7486 7888
www.apostropheuk.com
info@apostropheuk.com

RATING.

COFFEE
3.75 / 5

OVERALL
3.75 / 5

5

Caffè Nero Bedford St

10 Bedford Street, WC2E 7HE ....

OPEN.

Mon-Fri. 6:30am - 9:00pm
Sat. 7:30am - 9:00pm
Sun. 8:30am - 8:00pm

This Caffè Nero store, located in a stately old building on a busy corner in the middle of Charing Cross and Covent Garden, is a convenient stop for tourists on the well-trodden path around the West End. The simple interior, with its wooden finishings and high ceilings, provides a comfortable place to recharge, rest up and enjoy the Caffè Nero traditional Italian coffee experience.

FOOD.

Iced drinks, sandwiches, soups, pastas, salads, cakes, muffins, biscuits and pastries.

CONTACT.

+44(0)20 7240 9399
www.caffenero.com
enquires@caffenero.com

Sister coffee shops.
Over 400 UK outlets

OVERVIEW.

Catergory
Chain
Owner
Caffè Nero Group Ltd
First opened
2002

COFFEE & EQUIPMENT.

Coffee roaster
Caffè Nero
Coffee machine
Faema E91 Ambassador, 4 groups
Coffee grinder
Mazzer Super Jolly

COFFEE PRICING.

Espresso	£1.40 / £1.70		
Cappucino	£1.75 / £2.15 / £2.45		
Latte	£1.75 / £2.15 / £2.45		

RATING.

COFFEE 4.00 / 5	🫘 🫘 🫘 🫘 🫘
OVERALL 4.00 / 5	★ ★ ★ ★ ☆

Costa Coffee Great Portland Street

4 Great Portland Street, W1W 8QJ ....

Image supplied by Costa Coffee

OPEN.

Mon-Fri.	7:00am - 10:00pm
Sat.	8:00am - 10:00pm
Sun.	9:00am - 6:00pm

This brand new Costa Coffee store takes a large step away from the chain's usual branding and decor. It has a modern, stylish design with grey, red and yellow colours dominating. The interior boasts a mixture of textures including painted brick, distressed wood, and a funky feature wall of brightly coloured flowers. Seating is a combination of benches, communal and private tables, and a secluded nook in the corner. Already a very popular choice just a stone's throw from Oxford Circus.

FOOD.

Costa Coffee sandwiches, cakes, muffins and cookies

CONTACT.

+44(0)20 7436 7325
www.costa.co.uk
customer.relations@whitbread.com

Sister coffee shops.
Over 1000 in the UK

OVERVIEW.

Catergory
Chain
Owner
Whitbread PLC
First opened
2010

COFFEE & EQUIPMENT.

Coffee roaster
Costa Coffee
Coffee machine
Costa Coffee Marisa, 3 groups x 2
Coffee grinder
Mazzer

COFFEE PRICING.

Espresso	£1.35 / £1.70
Cappucino	£2.05 / £2.35 / £2.55
Latte	£2.05 / £2.35 / £2.55
Flat white	£2.25

RATING.

COFFEE 4.00 / 5

OVERALL 4.00 / 5

7

Joe & The Juice Regent Street
281 Regent Street, W1B 2HE

This is the first UK venture for well-established Danish chain Joe & The Juice. As the name suggests, this entertaining venue combines an extensive coffee menu and a range of delicious fresh juices.

The charming staff, comfy sofas and large upstairs loungeroom-style area make this the perfect place to escape the hustle and bustle of the West End. Come and see this vibrant newcomer for yourself.

Sister coffee shops.
Broadwick Street / 15 in Denmark / 1 in Sweden

Menu board:
- COFFEE OVERLOAD 3 SHOTS +35p
- ESPRESSEO 1.55
- DOUBLE ESPRESSO 1.90
- MACCHIATO 2.05
- CAPPUCCINO 2.50
- CUP OF JOE 1.80
- "TURKEY" turkey, mozzarella, tomato 4.25
- "TUNACADO" avocado, tuna mix 4.45
- "JOE'S CLUB" chicken, avocado, tomato 4.45
- All of JOE'S sandwiches are made with our own homemade pesto!
- EXTRA TOPPING +50p avocado, serrano, mozzarella, tomato, jalapeño, turkey, chicken, tabasco, tuna mousse

OPEN.

Mon-Fri.	7:30am - 9:00pm
Sat.	9:00am - 8:00pm
Sun.	10:00am - 8:00pm

OVERVIEW.

Catergory
Chain
Owner
Morten Basse and
Joe & The Juice RS Ltd
Head barista
Pippo
First opened
2009

COFFEE & EQUIPMENT.

Coffee roaster
Coffee Cartel
Coffee machine
La Marzocco Mistral, 2 groups
Coffee grinder
Mahlkönig

COFFEE PRICING.

Espresso	£1.55 / £1.80
Cappucino	£2.40
Latte	£1.90 / £2.10 / £2.30 / £2.60
Flat white	£2.30

FOOD.

A tempting selection of fresh and
colourful home-made paninis,
sandwiches and juices made
to order

CONTACT.

+44(0)77 9518 1673
www.joejuice.com
morty@joejuice.com

RATING.

COFFEE	
4.00 / 5	🫘 🫘 🫘 🫘 🫘
OVERALL	
4.50 / 5	★ ★ ★ ★ ⯪

9

Kaffeine

66 Great Titchfield Street, W1W 7QJ

Kaffeine has rapidly made its mark in the London coffee scene since opening in the summer of 2009. Peter sets the bar high and his team strive to provide the best café experience possible, whether you are new to coffee drinking or have tried it all before. Kaffeine has a welcoming, Antipodean feel and careful attention to detail is evident throughout, from the stylish café design to the latte art on each lovingly crafted coffee. It's easy to see why Kaffeine has already developed such a loyal following, which continues to grow as word spreads about this Fitzrovian gem. Winner of Best Independent Coffee Shop in Europe 2010, as voted by industry peers.

OPEN.

Mon-Fri.	7:30am-6:00pm
Sat.	9:00am-6:00pm
Sun.	Closed

OVERVIEW.

Catergory
Artisanal Independent
Owner
Peter Dore-Smith
Head barista
Catherine Seay
First opened
2009

COFFEE & EQUIPMENT.

Coffee roaster
Square Mile Coffee Roasters
Coffee machine
Synesso Cyncra, 3 groups
Coffee grinder
Mazzer Robur E

COFFEE PRICING.

Espresso	£1.50 / £2.00
Cappucino	£2.40
Latte	£2.40
Flat white	£2.30

FOOD.

Fresh salads, foccaccias, baguettes, pastries and cookies all made on site. Be sure to sample a blondie!

CONTACT.

+44(0)20 7580 6755
www.kaffeine.co.uk
peter@kaffeine.co.uk

RATING.

COFFEE
4.75 / 5

OVERALL
4.75 / 5

La Fromagerie Marylebone

2-6 Moxon Street, W1U 4EW

The enticing aroma is enough to draw any cheese lover up the street and inside the door of this wonderful fromagerie, deli and café. Along with a dazzling array of cheese, the interior is bursting with all manner of chutneys, jam, fruit, wine and other assorted home-made goodies for sale. The food is fresh and seasonal, locally-sourced wherever possible. Choose from breakfast, hearty lunch or cakes and pastries to accompany your coffee pulled from a beautifully maintained Faema.

Sister coffee shops.
Highbury Barn

OPEN.

Mon-Fri.	8:00am - 7:30pm
Sat.	9:00am - 7:00pm
Sun.	10:00am - 6:00pm

(During August closes 6:30pm Mon-Thu)

OVERVIEW.

Catergory
Artisanal Independent
Owner
Patricia Michelson
First opened
2002

COFFEE & EQUIPMENT.

Coffee roaster
Le Piantagioni Del Caffe
Coffee machine
Faema E61 Legend, 2 groups
Coffee grinder
Mazzer Super Jolly

COFFEE PRICING.

Espresso	£1.80 / £2.00
Cappucino	£2.80
Latte	£2.80
Flat white	£2.80

FOOD.

Croissants, pastries, hot lunch specials and afternoon tea to eat in, or a staggering choice of fresh produce to take away

CONTACT.

+44(0)20 7935 0341
www.lafromagerie.co.uk
moxon@lafromagerie.co.uk

RATING.

COFFEE 3.75 / 5	🫘 🫘 🫘 🫘 🫘
OVERALL 3.75 / 5	★ ★ ★ ⯪ ☆

Lantana

13 Charlotte Place, W1T 1SN ··

Stylish and modern without being pretentious, Lantana is a social meeting point for the hipster crowd and local workers alike. There is always a lively buzz and the café is busy at any time of day. The coffee here is of a consistently high quality – demand has been so great that Shelagh has opened a second shop front next door just to cater for the take-away traffic. Lantana is one of the main players in the happening Fitzrovian café scene.

Sister coffee shops.
Lantana Out (next door)

OPEN.

Mon-Wed. 8:00am - 6:00pm
Thu-Fri. 8:00am - 9:00pm
Sat-Sun. 9:00am - 5:00pm

OVERVIEW.

Catergory
Artisanal Independent
Owner
Shelagh Ryan
Head barista
Sean Gallagher
First opened
2008

COFFEE & EQUIPMENT.

Coffee roaster
Monmouth Coffee Company
Coffee machine
La Marzocco Linea, 3 groups
Coffee grinder
Anfim, Mazzer Super Jolly

COFFEE PRICING.

Espresso	£1.40 / £1.60
Cappucino	£2.40
Latte	£2.40
Flat white	£2.40

FOOD.

An appealing range of fresh
and healthy salads, sandwiches
and soups follow on from the
breakfast menu

CONTACT.

+44(0)20 7637 3347
www.lantanacafe.co.uk
shelagh.ryan@gmail.com

RATING.

COFFEE
4.50 / 5

OVERALL
4.50 / 5

Monmouth Coffee Company

27 Monmouth Street, WC2H 9EU

This is where the Monmouth phenomenon began, back in 1978. The original Monmouth roastery occupied this site until 2007 when it moved to Bermondsey after outgrowing the premises. The revamped interior here is small, homely and simple, keeping the focus on the coffee. Wooden communal booths encourage strangers to share space and a chat (no mobile phones allowed!). Monmouth Coffee is nothing short of exceptional, each shot expertly pulled and topped with exquisite latte art. More often than not, queues of people snake out the door onto the pavement, but it's definitely worth the wait.

Covent Garden

OPEN.

Mon-Sat. 8:00am - 6:30pm
Sun. Closed

OVERVIEW.

Catergory
Artisanal Independent
Owner
Anita Le Roy
First opened
1978

COFFEE & EQUIPMENT.

Coffee roaster
Monmouth Coffee Company
Coffee machine
La Marzocco Linea, 2 groups x 2
Coffee grinder
Mazzer

COFFEE PRICING.

Espresso	£1.30 / £1.80
Cappucino	£2.30
Latte	£2.30
Flat white	£2.30

Sister coffee shops.
The Borough / Bermondsey

Also serve **single origin filter coffee**. Coffee is roasted at Monmouth Coffee Company roastery in Bermondsey

FOOD.

A selection of pastries, croissants, cakes and tarts are displayed on the counter by the entrance

CONTACT.

+44(0)20 7379 3516
www.monmouthcoffee.co.uk
beans@monmouthcoffee.co.uk

RATING.

COFFEE
4.75 / 5

OVERALL
4.25 / 5

Napket Piccadilly

61 Piccadilly, W1J 0DY ....

Napket is the destination of choice for London's fashionable crowd.
A chic and stylish venue in the heart of Mayfair, Napket offers a decadent place for a special lunch out or evening date. The food and service is continental-style, complemented by Illy coffee. Step inside Napket to escape the crowds in luxurious surrounds.

FOOD.

Cakes, sandwiches, croissants, salads and pasta

CONTACT.

+44(0)20 7493 4704
www.napket.com
61@napket.com

Sister coffee shops.
Regent Street / Hanover Square / City / Chelsea / Kuwait

OVERVIEW.

Catergory
Designer
Owner
Eric Hanson
First opened
2007

COFFEE & EQUIPMENT.

Coffee roaster
Illy
Coffee machine
Chambali
Coffee grinder
Illy

COFFEE PRICING.

Espresso	£1.75	£2.55
Cappucino	£2.55	£3.15
Latte	£2.55	£3.15

RATING.

COFFEE 3.50 / 5	🫘 🫘 🫘 🫘 🫘
OVERALL 4.25 / 5	★ ★ ★ ★ ☆

Notes, Music & Coffee

31 St Martin's Lane, WC2N 4ER ....

OPEN.

Mon-Fri.	7:30am - 9:00pm
Sat.	8:30am - 9:00pm
Sun.	10:00am - 5:30pm

Notes, Music & Coffee is the brand new venture from Brazilian coffee entrepreneur Fabio Fereira. The coffee shop features a bar-style coffee serverie amongst an extensive audio-visual library of music and movies. Located in the heart of London's theatre district, this classy new venue is a great option for a coffee break in the West End, by day or by night.

FOOD.

A variety of fresh salads, sandwiches and sweet treats home-made on site

CONTACT.

+44(0)20 7240 0424
www.notesmusiccoffee.com

Sister Coffee Shops.
Flat Cap Coffee Co. (Stall)

OVERVIEW.

Catergory
Artisanal Independent
Owner / Head barista
Fabio Ferreira
First Opened
2010

HARDWARE.

Coffee roaster
Square Mile Coffee Roasters,
Has Bean Coffee
Coffee machine
La Marzocco Strada, 3 group
Coffee grinder
Mazzer Rober, Mahlkönig

COFFEE.

Espresso	£1.50 / £2.00
Cappucino	£2.50
Latte	£2.50
Flat white	£2.50

RATING.

COFFEE 4.50 / 5	🫘🫘🫘🫘🫘
OVERALL 4.25 / 5	★★★★★

Patisserie Valerie Marylebone

105 Marylebone High Street, W1U 4RS ·······································

OPEN.

Mon-Fri.	7:30am - 7:00pm
Sat.	8:00am - 7:00pm
Sun.	8:30am - 6:00pm

This Patisserie Valerie store is something of a Marylebone instution. Inside, the focal point is the watercolour murals adorning the walls, transporting you to the continental Europe of days gone by. There are plenty of delectable sweet treats for you to enjoy with an Illy coffee, or try something heartier from the all-day breakfast menu.

FOOD.

Famous for its French patisserie cakes, croissants and treats; also serve continental breakfast, brunch and specialty sandwiches

CONTACT.

+44(0)20 7935 6240
www.patisserie-valerie.co.uk
marylebone@valeriecafe.co.uk

Sister coffee shops.
33 UK locations

OVERVIEW.

Catergory
Chain
Owner
Patisserie Holdings Ltd
First opened
1993

COFFEE & EQUIPMENT.

Coffee roaster
Illy
Coffee machine
Fracino, 3 groups
Coffee grinder
Mazzer srl Super Jolly

COFFEE PRICING.

Espresso	£1.70 / £2.50
Cappucino	£2.60
Latte	£2.60

RATING.

COFFEE	3.50 / 5
OVERALL	3.75 / 5

The Providores

109 Marylebone High Street, W1U 4RX ·······································

OPEN.

Mon-Fri.	9:00am - 11:00pm
Sat.	10:00am - 11:00pm
Sun.	10:00am - 10:30pm

Run by New Zealand chef Peter Gordon, The Providores is a classy eatery on upmarket Marylebone High St. The ground floor Tapa Room, named after the striking bark tapa cloth occupying one wall, is heaving with people from breakfast through to dinner. A Monmouth special blend is the coffee of choice, perfect to accompany the delicious breakfast offerings (available til 3pm on weekends). Staff are cheerful and welcoming, the atmosphere warm and vibrant. The formal dining room upstairs is open for lunch and dinner.

FOOD.

"Fusion food" - a delectable breakfast menu, tapas for sharing and heartier mains

CONTACT.

+44(0)20 7935 6175
www.theprovidores.co.uk
anyone@theprovidores.co.uk

OVERVIEW.

Catergory
Eatery
Owner
Peter Gordon and Michael McGrath
Head Barista
Melanie Ellis
First Opened
2001

COFFEE & EQUIPMENT.

Coffee roaster
Monmouth Coffee Company
Coffee machine
La Marzocco GB5, 2 groups
Coffee grinder
Macin Adolsatore,
Mazzer Super Jolly

COFFEE PRICING.

Espresso	£2.00 / £2.40
Cappucino	£2.80
Latte	£2.80
Flat white	£2.80

RATING.

COFFEE 4.50 / 5

OVERALL 4.50 / 5 ★★★★⯪

Reynolds Charlotte Street

53 Charlotte Street, W1T 4PA

OPEN.

Mon-Fri.	8:00am-6:00pm
Sat-Sun.	Closed

Reynolds is a fresh and upbeat eatery and coffee shop in London's West End. The owners are strong believers in reusing and recycling - the back wall is made of old packing crates, the lights are genuine vintage from an old factory, and regular customers are rewarded for reusing their paper take away bags and coffee sleeves. The space is welcoming and communal, and art exhibitions on the walls rotate monthly to keep things interesting.

FOOD.

A 'grazing' menu featuring smaller portions of wraps, sandwiches and salads - share amongst friends or try a few for yourself

CONTACT.

+44(0)20 7580 0730
www.letsgrazereynolds.co.uk
hello@letsgrazereynolds.co.uk

Sister coffee shops.
Eastcastle Street

OVERVIEW.

Catergory
Eatery
Owner
Ben Reynolds
Head barista
Jess
First opened
2009

COFFEE & EQUIPMENT.

Coffee roaster
Union Hand-Roasted
Coffee machine
Nuevo Simonelli, 2 groups
Coffee grinder
Mazzer

COFFEE PRICING.

Espresso	£1.30 / £1.50
Cappucino	£2.00
Latte	£2.00
Flat white	£2.00

RATING.

COFFEE 3.75 / 5

OVERALL 3.75 / 5

Starbucks Conduit Street
2-3 Conduit Street, W1S 2BX ....

Image supplied by Starbucks

OPEN.

Mon-Fri.	6:30am - 10:00pm
Sat.	7:00am - 10:00pm
Sun.	7:00am - 8:00pm

This Conduit Street concept store scales back the usual Starbucks branding in favour of a more subtle approach. Wooden, earthy tones dominate, replacing the standard dark green tones and helping to create a more relaxing environment. The basement is an open space with a loungeroom feel; there are private areas for business meetings or simply to gossip and unwind.

FOOD.

Signature Starbucks sandwiches, paninis, muffins and cakes

CONTACT.

+44(0)20 7493 9754
www.starbucks.co.uk
ukinfo@starbucks.com

Sister coffee shops.
Approximately 300 stores in London

OVERVIEW.

Catergory
Chain
Owner
Starbucks Corporation
First opened
2009

COFFEE & EQUIPMENT.

Coffee roaster
Starbucks Roast
Coffee machine
Mastrena
Coffee grinder
Ditting

COFFEE PRICING.

Espresso	£1.40 / £1.65
Cappucino	£2.10 / £2.40 / £2.70
Latte	£2.10 / £2.40 / £2.70
Flat white	£2.35

RATING.

COFFEE 4.00 / 5	🫘 🫘 🫘 🫘 🫘
OVERALL 4.25 / 5	★ ★ ★ ★ ⯪

Tapped & Packed

26 Rathbone Place, W1T 1JD

Freshly opened and already creating a huge buzz, Tapped & Packed offers Londoners a unique coffee experience. Alongside a selection of espresso blends, an ever-changing menu of brewed coffee from artisanal roasters is available. Select your coffee of choice and preferred brewing method (filter, cafetiere, siphon or aeropress) – but don't be overwhelmed, the knowledgeable baristas are more than happy to help you decide. Come along to try something new and learn about the artistry of coffee.

 decaf GF SOYA

OPEN.

Mon-Fri.	8:00am - 7:00pm
Sat.	9:00am - 6:00pm
Sun.	Closed

OVERVIEW.

Catergory
Artisanal Independent
Owner
Richard Lilley
Head barista
Victor Frankowski
First opened
2010

COFFEE & EQUIPMENT.

Coffee roaster
Climpson & Sons, Square Mile
Coffee Roasters, Union Hand-
Roasted, Has Bean Coffee and Origin
Coffee machine
Nuevo Simonelli Aurelia, 4 groups,
Aeropress
Coffee grinder
Mazzer Rober E, Mazzer Super Jolly,
Anfim Super Caimano Timed, DIP
Deli Grinder

COFFEE PRICING.

Espresso	£1.20 / £1.50
Cappucino	£2.20
Latte	£2.20
Flat white	£2.20

FOOD.

Gourmet breakfast, all-day pastries,
cakes and chocolates

CONTACT.

+44(0)20 7580 2163
www.tappedandpacked.co.uk
postmaster@tappedandpacked.co.uk

As well as espresso-based coffee,
Tapped & Packed specialise in
**brewed coffee (filter, cafetiere,
siphon and AeroPress)**

RATING.

COFFEE 4.75 / 5	🫘 🫘 🫘 🫘 🫘
OVERALL 4.75 / 5	★ ★ ★ ★ ★

Soho

Soho, London's nightlife and entertainment hub, is buzzing with people day and night. The home of the first espresso bar to open in London, Soho has always been at the forefront of UK coffee culture and is now the epicentre of the 'third wave' artisanal coffee scene.

....

Soho

Bar Italia
22 Frith Street, W1D 4RP

TOP
30

OPEN.
Mon-Sun. Open 24 hours

One of London's oldest (and most famous) coffee shops, Bar Italia has been a Soho institution since 1949. Inside, the walls are covered with framed photographs of a selection of the famous showbiz clientele who have frequented the venue over the years. Open all hours, this is the place for a pick-me up authentic Italian coffee after a long night out clubbing or treading the boards, when all the sensible people are at home in bed.

FOOD.
Traditional Italian fare

CONTACT.
+44(0)20 7437 4520
www.baritaliasoho.co.uk
info@baritaliasoho.co.uk

OVERVIEW.
Catergory
Eatery
Owner
Antonio Pollederi
First opened
1949

COFFEE & EQUIPMENT.
Coffee roaster
Italian Roaster
Coffee machine
Gaggia, 2 groups
Coffee grinder
Mazzer

COFFEE PRICING.
Espresso	£2.00 / £3.20
Cappucino	£2.70 / £3.20
Latte	£2.80 / £3.50

RATING.

COFFEE 4.25 / 5	🌰🌰🌰🌰🌗
OVERALL 4.25 / 5	★★★★✦

Brewed Boy Espresso

Pitch 1202, Rupert Street Market, W1D ....

OPEN.
Mon-Fri. 8:00am - 3:30pm

Rob Lockyear created Brewed Boy Espresso in early 2010 and has made a home for his charming cart at the Rupert St Market in Soho. Serving Square Mile coffee to locals and tourists alike, Brewed Boy keeps it simple and delivers a quality brew with a smile and a friendly chat. Browse his small book exchange while you wait, and soak up the quirky atmosphere of the market and surrounding streets.

FOOD.

A selection of handmade croissants and cakes

CONTACT.

+44(0)75 5259 1125
brewedboy@gmail.com

Sister coffee shops.
Cabbages and Frocks Market
(Saturdays)

OVERVIEW.

Catergory
Stall / Cart / Kiosk
Owner / Head barista
Rob Lockyear
First opened
2010

COFFEE & EQUIPMENT.

Coffee roaster
Square Mile Coffee Roasters
Coffee machine
Bezzera, 2 groups
Coffee grinder
Anfim

COFFEE PRICING.

Espresso	£1.20 / £1.50
Cappucino	£2.20
Latte	£2.20
Flat white	£2.20

RATING.

COFFEE
4.25 / 5

Fernandez & Wells Café

73 Beak Street, W1F 9SR

OPEN.

Mon-Fri.	7:30am - 6:00pm
Sat.	9:00am - 6:00pm
Sun.	10:00am - 6:00pm

Fernandez & Wells Café was one of the first establishments in central London to combine gourmet deli food and a love of quality coffee. The business has expanded to include a deli and an espresso bar, both within close walking distance. The café has a rustic, country feel with cream walls, timber benches and a simple layout. Passionate about coffee, the knowledgeable baristas take pride in every pour from the gleaming Synesso Cyncra.

FOOD.

An alluring spread of sandwiches, baguettes and deli-style goodies is beautifully presented on stone benches

CONTACT.

+44(0)20 7287 8124
www.fernandezandwells.com
taste@fernandezandwells.com

Sister coffee shops.
Fernandez & Wells Espresso Bar

OVERVIEW.

Catergory
Artisanal Independent
Owner
Jorge Fernandez and Rick Wells
Head barista
Kat Ross
First opened
2007

COFFEE & EQUIPMENT.

Coffee roaster
Has Bean Coffee
Coffee machine
Synesso Cyncra, 3 groups
Coffee grinder
Mazzer Robur, Mazzer Robur E

COFFEE PRICING.

Espresso	£2.20
Cappucino	£2.50
Latte	£2.50
Flat white	£2.50

RATING.

| COFFEE 4.75 / 5 | |
| OVERALL 4.50 / 5 | |

Fernandez & Wells Espresso Bar

16a St. Anne's Court, W1F 0BG ....

OPEN.

Mon.	8:00am-6:00pm
Tue.-Wed.	8:00am-8:00pm
Thu.-Fri.	8:00am-10:00pm
Sat.	9:00pm-6:00pm
Sun.	Closed

The newest offering from the Fernandez & Wells team is tucked away in a small Soho side street. With a row of bench seating occupying one wall, the space is small but functional. The quality and attention to detail that are signatures of the Fernandez & Wells Café are apparent here, with a more casual vibe. This venue is open into the evenings as a wine bar.

FOOD.

Chunky baguettes, warming stews, soups and other appealing choices from the Fernandez & Wells deli

CONTACT.

+44(0)20 7494 4242
www.fernandezandwells.com
taste@fernandezandwells.com

Sister coffee shops.
Fernandez & Wells Café

OVERVIEW.

Catergory
Artisanal Independent
Owner
Jorge Fernandez and Rick Wells
Head barista
David Robson and Joe Lawrence
First opened
2009

COFFEE & EQUIPMENT.

Coffee roaster
Has Bean Coffee
Coffee machine
Synesso Cyncra, 3 groups
Coffee grinder
Mazzer Robur, Mazzer Robur E

COFFEE PRICING.

Espresso	£2.20
Cappucino	£2.50
Latte	£2.50
Flat white	£2.50

RATING.

| COFFEE 4.50 / 5 | OVERALL 4.25 / 5 |

Flat White

17 Berwick Street, W1F 0PT

Flat White was opened in 2005 with the aim of introducing the Antipodean café scene to London, and is viewed as a pioneer of the third wave coffee movement.
A mecca for Kiwis and Aussies longing for a touch of home - and for curious Londoners wondering what all the fuss is about - Flat White is grungy and unpretentious but always buzzing. Come and experience it for yourself, but arrive early to secure a seat as space is very limited!

Sister coffee shops.
Milkbar

OPEN.

Mon-Fri. 8:00am - 7:00pm
Sat-Sun. 9:00am - 6:00pm

OVERVIEW.

Catergory
Artisanal Independent
Owner
Cameron McClure and Peter Hall
First opened
2005

COFFEE & EQUIPMENT.

Coffee roaster
Square Mile Coffee Roasters
Coffee machine
La Marzocco Linea, 2 groups x 2
Coffee grinder
Mazzer Robur E, Mazzer Decaf

COFFEE PRICING.

Espresso	£1.80 / £2.30
Cappucino	£2.50
Latte	£2.50
Flat white	£2.50

FOOD.

Made-to-order salads, chunky
sandwiches, caff-style all day menu

CONTACT.

+44(0)20 7734 0370
flattie@flat-white.co.uk

RATING.

COFFEE 4.75 / 5	🫘🫘🫘🫘🫘
OVERALL 4.50 / 5	★★★★⯪

Foxcroft & Ginger

3 Berwick Street, W1F 0DR

OPEN.
Mon-Fri. 8:00am - 7:00pm
Sat-Sun. 9:00am - 7:00pm

Enter through the heavy wooden door into one of Soho's newest coffee scene offerings. The mood inside is industrial meets rural, with rustic wooden floors, a mixture of concrete, tile and brick walls and exposed piping on the ceilings. The pommel horse and eclectic furniture pieces downstairs are great conversation-starters. Smooth and rich Monmouth Coffee is pulled from a shiny new Synesso Cyncra.

FOOD.

Fresh salads, croissants, baguettes and cakes are made on site from locally sourced produce

CONTACT.

+44(0)20 7644 6348
www.foxcroftandginger.co.uk
info@foxcroftandginger.co.uk

OVERVIEW.

Catergory
Artisanal Independent
Owner
Quintin Dawson
Head barista
Nfa Jones
First opened
2010

COFFEE & EQUIPMENT.

Coffee roaster
Monmouth Coffee Company
Coffee machine
Synesso Cyncra, 3 groups
Coffee grinder
Anfim

COFFEE PRICING.

Espresso	£1.70
Cappucino	£2.20
Latte	£2.20
Flat white	£2.20

RATING.

COFFEE 4.00 / 5
OVERALL 3.75 / 5

Joe & The Juice Broadwick Street

65 Broadwick Street, W1F 9QU ....

OPEN.

Mon-Fri.	7:30am - 8:00pm
Sat.	9:00am - 7:00pm
Sun.	10:00am - 7:00pm

Joe & The Juice recently opened their second London venture in Soho. Smaller than its Regent Street counterpart, it promotes the same lively atmosphere, with loud funky music and staff who seem to be enjoying themselves far too much for people who are at work. A fun place to drop in for your morning pick-me-up coffee or a tasty lunchtime panini.

FOOD.

A tempting selection of fresh and colourful home-made paninis, sandwiches and juices made to order

CONTACT.

+44(0)77 9518 1673
www.joejuice.com
morty@joejuice.com

Sister coffee shops.
Regent Street / 15 in Denmark / 1 in Sweden

OVERVIEW.

Catergory
Chain
Owner
Morten Basse and
Joe and the Juice RS Ltd
First opened
2010

COFFEE & EQUIPMENT.

Coffee roaster
Coffee Cartel
Coffee machine
La Marzocco GB5, 2 groups
Coffee grinder
Mahlkönig

COFFEE PRICING.

Espresso	£1.55 / £1.80
Cappucino	£2.40
Latte	£1.90 / £2.10 / £2.30 / £2.60
Flat white	£2.30

RATING.

COFFEE 4.00 / 5

OVERALL 4.00 / 5

LJ Coffee House

3 Winnett Street, W1D 6JY ....

The overwhelming feel upon entering LJ Coffee House is that you've just wandered into someone's living room. David Littlejohn has succeeded in creating a community environment in his small gem of a coffee house, in the heart of the busy theatre district. Everyone is welcome (even dogs) and encouraged to settle in on the couch and linger all day long. David is passionate about coffee and this is evident in every cup served here.

OPEN.

Mon-Tue.	7:30am - 7:00pm
Wed-Fri.	7:30am - 9:00pm
Sat.	10:00am - 9:00pm
Sun.	1:00pm - 8:00pm

OVERVIEW.

Catergory
Artisanal Independent
Owner / Head barista
David Littlejohn
First opened
2008

COFFEE & EQUIPMENT.

Coffee roaster
Union Hand-Roasted
Coffee machine
La Marzocco GB5, 2 groups
Coffee grinder
Mazzer Luigi Srl

COFFEE PRICING.

Espresso	£1.55 / £1.95
Cappucino	£2.25 / £2.60 / £2.95
Latte	£2.25 / £2.60 / £2.95
Flat white	£2.60

FOOD.

Outside-catered sandwiches, salads and cakes

CONTACT.

+44(0)20 7434 1174
www.ljcoffeehouse.org.uk
ljcoffeehouse@btconnect.com

RATING.

COFFEE	4.25 / 5	🫘🫘🫘🫘🫘
OVERALL	4.25 / 5	★★★★★

Milkbar

3 Bateman Street, W1D 4AG ....

Although comparisons to its sibling Flat White are inevitable, Milkbar is strong enough to stand on its own two feet. With exceptional coffee, an artsy, grungy feel and enough space for you to linger all day, Milkbar is the kind of hangout joint you wish was your local. Proudly Antipodean, Milkbar offers an all-day breakfast/ brunch menu and a space for rotating local art exhibitions.

Sister coffee shops.
Flat White

OPEN.

Mon-Fri.   8:00am - 7:00pm
Sat-Sun.   9:00am - 6:00pm

OVERVIEW.

Catergory
Artisanal Independent
Owner
Cameron McClure
First opened
2008

COFFEE & EQUIPMENT.

Coffee roaster
Square Mile Coffee Roasters
Coffee machine
La Marzocco FB80, 3 groups
Coffee grinder
Anfirm, Mazzer Decaf

COFFEE PRICING.

Espresso	£1.80
Cappucino	£2.50
Latte	£2.50
Flat white	£2.50

FOOD.

All-day breakfast and brunch,
fresh salads, sandwiches and
sweet snacks

CONTACT.

+44(0)20 7287 4796
flattie@flat-white.co.uk

RATING.

COFFEE 4.75 / 5	🫘 🫘 🫘 🫘 🫘
OVERALL 4.50 / 5	★ ★ ★ ★ ½

Princi

135 Wardour Street, W1F 0UT ....

Sleek, stylish Princi is the first London outlet of an established Italian bakery chain, brought to this city by Alan Yau of Wagamama fame. A buzzing, lively eatery, Princi fits in effortlessy to Soho and is jam-packed all hours of the day and night. One length of the venue is occupied by tantalising displays of croissants, tarts, cakes, pizza and salads all freshly made on site. The elegant dining area consists of granite tables and a long metal bench against the beautiful water feature wall, and the large window frontage is great for people-watching on this entertaining street.

OPEN.

Mon-Sat. 7:00am-12:00am
Sun. 9:00am-10:00pm

OVERVIEW.

Catergory
Designer
Owner
Rocco Princi and Alan Yau
Head barista
Patrizia Putzolo
First opened
2008

COFFEE & EQUIPMENT.

Coffee roaster
Kontra
Coffee machine
La Marzocco Linea, 3 groups
Coffee grinder
Mahlkönig

Sister coffee shops.
4 Princi bakeries in Milan

COFFEE PRICING.

Espresso	£1.50
Cappucino	£2.20
Latte	£2.20
Flat white	£1.50

FOOD.

Pizzas baked in the stone oven, an endless array of pastries, plus a selection of salads and hot meals

CONTACT.

+44(0)20 7478 8888
www.princi.co.uk
email@princi.co.uk

RATING.

COFFEE 4.00 / 5	🫘 🫘 🫘 🫘 🫘
OVERALL 4.50 / 5	★ ★ ★ ★ ⯪

41

Sacred Ganton Street

13 Ganton Street, W1F 9BL ....

This is the original Sacred café, first opened in 2005. The owners are proud New Zealanders and this shines through in the decor, ambience and relaxed atmosphere they have created. The space is welcoming, with great vantage points to people watch and couches in the mellow basement area to make you feel at home. Take some time out from shopping on Carnaby St to enjoy a coffee here – you won't be disappointed.

Sister coffee shops.
Covent Garden / Highbury Studios / Westfield / Kingly Court / Torrington Street

Images supplied by Sacred

OPEN.

| Mon-Fri. | 7:30am - 8:00pm |
| Sat-Sun. | 10:00am - 7:00pm |

OVERVIEW.

Catergory
Chain
Owner
Tubbs Wanigasekera and Matt Clark
Head barista
Liz Douglas
First opened
2005

COFFEE & EQUIPMENT.

Coffee roaster
Sacred House Roast
Coffee machine
La Marzocco Linea, 2 groups
Coffee grinder
Mazzer

COFFEE PRICING.

Espresso	£1.60
Cappucino	£2.50 / £2.70
Latte	£2.50 / £2.70
Flat white	£2.50 / £2.70

FOOD.

All-day menu of breakfast, bagels, sandwiches, cakes and pastries

CONTACT.

+44(0)20 7734 1415
www.sacredcafe.co.uk
globalcoffee@gmail.com

RATING.

| COFFEE 4.25 / 5 | 🫘🫘🫘🫘🫘 |
| OVERALL 4.50 / 5 | ★★★★✬ |

for a consistently great soya latte or soyaccino

alpro soya®

www.alprosoya.co.

Farringdon & Clerkenwell

Traditionally an area dominated by breweries, meatworks and the printing industry, Farringdon & Clerkenwell is now an interesting combination of commercial premises, residences and industry. The area's rich Italian history is bound to influence its emerging boutique coffee and dining culture.

Brill
27 Exmouth Market, EC1R 4QL ....

The growth in online music and subsequent demise in CD sales presented Jeremy Brill with the perfect opportunity to re-invent his music store. Now incorporating a coffee shop and bagelry, Brill is an innovative store that manages to be both edgy and homely. Relax and debate the musical merits of the CDs on offer whilst enjoying a satisfying cup of Union coffee as sun streams in through the front window.

OPEN.

Mon-Fri. 7.30am - 6.00pm
Sat. 9:00am - 6.00pm
Sun. Closed

OVERVIEW.

Catergory
Retail & Leisure
Owner
Jeremy Brill
First opened
2006

COFFEE & EQUIPMENT.

Coffee roaster
Union Hand-Roasted
Coffee machine
La Marzocco Linea, 2 groups
Coffee grinder
Mazzer Super Jolly

COFFEE PRICING.

Espresso £1.20 / £1.60
Cappucino £2.00 / £2.30
Latte £2.00 / £2.30
Flat white £2.00 / £2.30

FOOD.

Made-to-order fresh bagels and a
selection of pastries

CONTACT.

+44(0)20 7833 9757
jeremy@clerkenwellmusic.co.uk

RATING.

COFFEE
4.00 / 5

OVERALL
3.75 / 5

Caravan

11-13 Exmouth Market, EC1R 4QD ··

There is a lot of industry buzz surrounding Caravan, a new coffee roastery and restaurant on Farringdon's Exmouth Market. It is a classy and modern place, particularly inviting on warm sunny days when the dining space spills out onto the pavement. Caravan coffee is roasted downstairs in a 12kg machine you can appreciate for yourself. There are plenty of mouth-watering options on the menu for a lazy weekend brunch or casual dinner. Come and see this lively new kid on the block for yourself.

Images supplied by Caravan

OPEN.

Mon-Fri.	8:00am - 12:00am
Sat.	10:00am - 12:00am
Sun.	10:00am - 4:00pm

OVERVIEW.

Catergory
Eatery
Owner
Chris Ammermann, Jedediah Coleman and Miles Kirby
Head barista
Chris Ammermann
First opened
2010

COFFEE & EQUIPMENT.

Coffee roaster
Caravan
Coffee machine
La Marzocco Linea, 3 groups
Coffee grinder
Anfim, Mazzer, Vario x 4

COFFEE PRICING.

Espresso	£1.60 / £1.80
Cappucino	£2.40
Latte	£2.40
Flat white	£2.40

FOOD.

An all-day fusion food menu offers plenty of delicious choices

Also serve single origin filter coffee. Caravan coffee is **roasted on site**, downstairs from the restaurant

CONTACT.

+44(0)20 7833 8115
www.caravanonexmouth.co.uk
coffee@caravanonexmouth.co.uk

RATING.

COFFEE
4.75 / 5

OVERALL
4.25 / 5

Dose Espresso

69 Long Lane, EC1A 9EJ

Dose Espresso is well recognised as a leader in coffee excellence and one of the main players in the artisanal coffee scene. James Phillips sets the standard here in his small but welcoming espresso bar, using a Square Mile seasonal roast and featuring a weekly guest espresso blend. Dose is well respected by many in the industry and it's not hard to see why.

OPEN.

Mon-Fri.	7:00am - 4:00pm
Sat.	9:00am - 1:00pm
Sun.	Closed

OVERVIEW.

Catergory
Artisanal Independent
Owner / Head barista
James Phillips
First opened
2009

COFFEE & EQUIPMENT.

Coffee roaster
Square Mile Coffee Roasters and
guest espresso from
various roasters
Coffee machine
La Marzocco FB-80, 3 groups,
AeroPress
Coffee grinder
Anfim Super Caimano, Anfim Best
and Mahlkönig Vario

COFFEE PRICING.

Espresso	£1.30 / £1.60
Cappucino	£2.20 / £2.60
Latte	£2.20 / £2.60
Flat white	£2.20 / £2.60

FOOD.

Small breakfast menu, freshly
prepared salads and sandwiches,
and an assortment of sweet treats

CONTACT.

+44(0)20 7600 0382
www.dose-espresso.com
james@dose-espresso.com

Also features brewed coffee,
'AeroPress of the week' and **guest
espresso** from regularly changing
UK and international roasters

RATING.

COFFEE 4.75 / 5	🫘 🫘 🫘 🫘 🫘
OVERALL 4.25 / 5	★ ★ ★ ★ ⯨

Farm Collective

91 Cowcross Street, EC1M 6BH

OPEN.
Mon-Fri. 7:00am - 3:30pm
Sat-Sun. Closed

The Farm Collective take pride in sourcing high quality fresh produce directly from British farms. The emphasis on quality extends to the coffee - consistently smooth Square Mile espresso pulled through a Synesso Syncra. A tantalising food display makes this a great destination for a quick drop-in or a lazy lunch.

FOOD.

'Honest British Food' - breakfast, gourmet sandwiches, mouth-watering baked goods and hearty hot pastries

CONTACT.

+44(0)20 7253 2142
www.farmcollective.com
craig@farmcollective.com

OVERVIEW.

Catergory
Artisanal Independent
Owner
Dominic Kamara and Craig Wills
First opened
2009

COFFEE & EQUIPMENT.

Coffee roaster
Square Mile Coffee Roasters
Coffee machine
Synesso Cyncra, 2 groups
Coffee grinder
Anfim

COFFEE PRICING.

Espresso	£1.55 / £1.95
Cappucino	£1.90 / £2.30
Latte	£1.90 / £2.30
Flat white	£2.10 / £2.40

RATING.

| COFFEE | 4.25 / 5 |
| OVERALL | 3.75 / 5 |

The Modern Pantry

47-48 St John's Square, EC1V 4JJ ....

OPEN.

Mon.	8:00am - 10:00pm
Tue-Fri.	8:00am - 11:00pm
Sat.	9:00am - 11:00pm
Sun.	10:00am - 10:00pm

The Modern Pantry is a classy establishment in the heart of Clerkenwell. Upstairs is a formal dining area while downstairs is a more casual affair, perfect for an afternoon coffee or relaxed lunch. The feel here is light and bright with soft finishings, large windows and ambient music playing in the background. Come here for a more elegant affair or when looking to impress.

FOOD.

An all-day menu of snacks, share plates and mains, or try to resist the mouth-watering weekend brunch menu

CONTACT.

+44(0)20 7553 9210
www.themodernpantry.co.uk
enquiries@themodernpantry.co.uk

OVERVIEW.

Catergory
Eatery
Owner
Anna Hansen
Head barista
Jonathon Benoliel
First opened
2008

COFFEE & EQUIPMENT.

Coffee roaster
Caravan
Coffee machine
La Marzocco Linea, 2 groups
Coffee grinder
Mazzer Luigi

COFFEE PRICING.

Espresso	£2.00
Cappucino	£2.40 / £2.80
Latte	£2.40 / £2.80
Flat white	£2.40 / £2.80

RATING.

COFFEE 4.00 / 5

OVERALL 3.75 / 5

Camden
& Islington

Islington in London's inner north
is an area of tremendous diversity
with a strong creative pulse.
The neighbouring borough of Camden
encompasses alternative Camden
Town and upmarket Primrose Hill.
There are enough coffee venues to
keep even the fussiest caffeine addict
happy in this region of London.

Bean About Town Kentish Town

Kentish Town Station, corner Kentish Town Road & Leighton Road, NW5 2AA ....

You may have noticed several Bean About Town coffee vans dotted around the City of London. The Kentish Town outlet has been around since 2005 and is a trusted favourite amongst locals and commuting workers seeking a quality caffeine hit. A simple set-up that delivers consistently great coffee.

FOOD.

A small selection of fresh pastries and biscuits.

CONTACT.

+44(0)20 3239 6432
www.beanabouttown.com
info@beanabouttown.com

Sister coffee shops.
Kensington Olympia / St Katharine Dock / Camden Lock / Dalston Kingsland / Clapham North

OPEN.

Mon-Fri. 7:00am - 7:00pm
Sat-Sun. 9:00am - 5:00pm

OVERVIEW.

Catergory
Stall / Cart / Kiosk
Owner
Olivier Vetter
Head barista
Mariusz Lewicki
First opened
2005

COFFEE & EQUIPMENT.

Coffee roaster
Monmouth Coffee Company
Coffee machine
Izzo Pompeii Lever, 2 groups
Coffee grinder
Mazzer Super Jolly

COFFEE PRICING.

Espresso	£1.50
Cappucino	£1.60 / £2.00 / £2.30
Latte	£1.60 / £2.00 / £2.30
Flat white	£1.60 / £2.00 / £2.30

Wednesday is Organic Day -
each week a different organic blend is used instead of the usual Monmouth espresso blend

RATING.

COFFEE
3.75 / 5

Bea's of Bloomsbury

44 Theobald's Road, WC1X 8NW

OPEN.

Mon-Fri.	8:00am - 7:00pm
Sat.	10:00am - 7:00pm
Sun.	12:00pm - 7:00pm

The selection of cakes and treats on display at Bea's is enough to make any sweet tooth go weak at the knees. Afternoon tea is available (as a take-away picnic if you prefer on a sunny day) and Bea's also do a range of savoury foods for lunch. The open kitchen at the rear is great for curious customers to see how it's done. Square Mile coffee pulled from a pair of La Marzoccos complements the sweet treats beautifully.

FOOD.

An overwhelming choice of cakes and sweets, plus a full lunch menu. Try the passionfruit or raspberry marshmallows, or an enormous chocolate meringue

CONTACT.

+44(0)20 7242 8330
www.beasofbloomsbury.com
contact@beasofbloomsbury.com

Sister coffee shops.
Watling Street

OVERVIEW.

Catergory
Bakery Coffee Shop
Owner
Bea Vo
Head barista
Kristina Johansson
First Opened
2008

> Also serve
> **AeroPress**
> brewed coffee

COFFEE & EQUIPMENT.

Coffee roaster
Square Mile Coffee Roasters
Coffee machine
La Marzocco FB-70, 4 groups and
La Marzocco Linea, 2 groups
Coffee grinder
Anfim, Mazzer

COFFEE PRICING.

Espresso	£1.60
Cappucino	£2.30 / £2.60
Latte	£2.30 / £2.60
Flat white	£2.30 / £2.60

RATING.

COFFEE	OVERALL
4.25 / 5	4.25 / 5

Coffee Circus
Camden Lock Village Market, NW1 8AH ....

OPEN.
Mon-Fri. 9:30am - 6:30pm
Sat-Sun. 9:30am - 7:00pm

Coffee Circus was first set up in a tuk-tuk in Camden Village Market in 2009. Now expanded, the stall has developed its own quirky character with sheltered platform seating and even a fully functional piano. The muliti-national European team serve Matthew Algie coffee with enthusiasm and attention to detail. The smaller tuk-tuk stall can now be found across the road at the Camden Stables.

FOOD.

Try a stroopwafel for a divine sweet accompaniment to your coffee

CONTACT.

+44(0)75 3409 6407
info@coffeecircus.co.uk

Sister coffee shops.
Camden Stables

OVERVIEW.

Catergory
Stall / Cart / Kiosk
Owner
Gediminas Siminavicius and Dainoras Petrauskas
Head barista
Rummy Keshet
First opened
2009

COFFEE & EQUIPMENT.

Coffee roaster
Matthew Algie, Union Hand-Roasted
Coffee machine
Elektra Barlume, 2 groups
Coffee grinder
Mazzer

COFFEE PRICING.

Espresso	£1.40
Cappucino	£2.00 / £2.20
Latte	£2.00 / £2.20
Flat white	£2.00

RATING.

COFFEE
4.25 / 5

The Espresso Room

31-35 Great Ormond Street, WC1N 3HZ ....

OPEN.

Mon-Fri. 7:30am - 5:00pm
Sat-Sun. Closed

OVERVIEW.

Catergory
Artisanal Independent
Owner
Ben Townsend
First opened
2009

COFFEE & EQUIPMENT.

Coffee roaster
Square Mile Coffee Roasters
Coffee machine
La Marzocco Linea, 2 groups
Coffee grinder
Mazzer Robur E

COFFEE PRICING.

Espresso	£1.50 / £1.80
Cappucino	£2.20 / £2.70
Latte	£2.20 / £2.70
Flat white	£2.20 / £2.70

FOOD.

A small selection of cakes and freshly made sandwiches

The Espresso Room is a simple concept: take a tiny shop front, add a La Marzocco espresso machine, Mazzer grinder, Square Mile coffee and an owner who is passionate and knowledgeable about his trade...and the result is consistently excellent coffee. Space may be limited in this espresso bar, but the venue's reputation is growing by the minute. If you go there once, it's guaranteed you'll return!

CONTACT.

+44(0)77 6071 4883
www.theespressoroom.com
info@theespressoroom.com

RATING.

COFFEE
4.75 / 5

OVERALL
4.25 / 5

Fix
161 Whitecross Street, EC1Y 8JL ....

Discreetly occupying a corner location adjacent to the Whitecross St Market, Fix is a spacious and funky place to drop in for a coffee and bite to eat. The big leather couches are usually occupied by artsy types on computers, reading or catching up on the latest gossip while upbeat music plays in the background. A great place to spend the afternoon relaxing with a warming cup of coffee.

OPEN.
Mon-Fri. 7:00am - 7:00pm
Sat-Sun. 8:00am - 7:00pm

OVERVIEW.
Catergory
Artisanal Independent
Owner
Alexander Reiney
First Opened
2009

COFFEE & EQUIPMENT.
Coffee roaster
Union Hand-Roasted
Coffee machine
Rancilio Classe 8, 3 groups
Coffee grinder
Mazzer Super Jolly

COFFEE PRICING.
Espresso £1.40 / £1.70
Cappucino £1.95 / £2.20 / £2.50
Latte £1.95 / £2.20 / £2.50
Flat white £1.95 / £2.20 / £2.50

FOOD.
Pre-made sandwiches and salads,
hearty soups and tempting
bakery treats

CONTACT.
+44(0)20 7490 8081
www.fix-coffee.co.uk
sashafixcoffee@gmail.com

RATING.
COFFEE 4.00 / 5
OVERALL 4.00 / 5

61

Fleet River Bakery

71 Lincoln's Inn Fields, WC2A 3JF

OPEN.

Mon-Fri.	7:00am - 6:00pm
Sat.	9:00am - 5:00pm
Sun.	Closed

Fleet River Bakery is tucked in beside the north-west corner of Lincoln's Inn Fields. Offering freshly baked sandwiches, quiches and other tasty treats alongside Monmouth Coffee, it is a lovely place to stop and unwind. The ground floor café quickly fills with Holborn office workers by lunchtime, while downstairs is more low key and provides a nice peaceful space for a meeting or to read a book. Check out the great photos on display throughout the venue.

FOOD.

Breakfast, fresh sandwiches and daily changing salads, quiches and baked treats all made on site

CONTACT.

+44(0)20 7691 1457
www.fleetriverbakery.com
info@fleetriverbakery.com

OVERVIEW.

Catergory
Bakery Coffee Shop
Owner
Jon Dalton
Head barista
Joseph, Stef and Kerryn
First opened
2009

COFFEE & EQUIPMENT.

Coffee roaster
Monmouth Coffee Company
Coffee machine
La Marzocco Linea, 3 groups
Coffee grinder
Anfim

COFFEE PRICING.

Espresso	£1.30 / £1.50
Cappucino	£2.10
Latte	£2.10
Flat white	£2.10

RATING.

COFFEE 4.00 / 5	🫘🫘🫘🫘🫘
OVERALL 3.75 / 5	★★★★★

Ginger & White

4a-5a Perrins Court, NW3 1QS

OPEN.
Mon-Fri. 7:30am - 5:30pm
Sat-Sun. 8:30am - 5:30pm

Proudly British, this café wears its heart on its sleeve. A local gem ever-popular with the Hampstead community, Ginger & White serve a well-crafted Square Mile coffee alongside modern British meals made from locally-sourced produce. With a communal dining table and window seats to watch the world go by, this is a great place to enjoy a leisurely brunch.

FOOD.

Locally sourced British food - all-day breakfast, seasonal sarnies, fresh salads and home-made cakes

CONTACT.

+44(0)20 7431 9098
www.gingerandwhite.com
info@gingerandwhite.com

OVERVIEW.

Catergory
Eatery
Owner
Tonia George, Nicholas and Emma Scott
Head barista
Mai Wang
First opened
2009

COFFEE & EQUIPMENT.

Coffee roaster
Square Mile Coffee Roasters
Coffee machine
La Marzocco Linea, 3 groups
Coffee grinder
Anfim, Mazzer

COFFEE PRICING.

Espresso	£1.70 / £2.30
Cappucino	£2.30
Latte	£2.30
Flat white	£2.30

RATING.

COFFEE 4.50 / 5	
OVERALL 4.25 / 5	

Goswell Road Coffee

160-164 Goswell Road, EC1V 7DU ....

OPEN.

Mon-Fri.	7:00am - 7:00pm
Sat-Sun.	8:00am - 7:00pm

Goswell Road Coffee is another Street Coffee venture, and has a similar feel to its two counterparts. Ethica coffee is again the focal point – you can 'pimp your ride' with extra shots or flavourings, or stick to 'chav coffee' (filter coffee). A hip place to hang out with friends, surf the internet or read a book. Check out the clever lampshades made from old coffee cups and milk bottles.

FOOD.

A selection of sandwiches, soups and snacks

CONTACT.

+44(0)20 7490 7444
jaysinstreetcoffee@gmail.com

Sister coffee shops.
Brick Lane / Bermondsey Street

OVERVIEW.

Catergory
Chain
Owner
Street Coffee / Adrian Jones
Head barista
Jaysin Degiorgio
First opened
2009

COFFEE & EQUIPMENT.

Coffee roaster
Ethica Coffee
Coffee machine
Rancilio Classe 8, 3 groups
Coffee grinder
Mazzer Super Jolly

COFFEE PRICING.

Espresso	£1.70 / £1.50
Cappucino	£2.00 / £2.35 / £2.70
Latte	£2.00 / £2.35 / £2.70
Flat white	£2.00 / £2.35 / £2.70

RATING.

COFFEE	
4.00 / 5	
OVERALL	
4.00 / 5	

Lanka

71 Regents Park Road, NW1 8UY

OPEN.

Mon-Fri.   9:00am - 7:00pm
Sat-Sun.   8:00am - 7:00pm

(Jan-Mar: Mon-Sun. 9:00am - 5:00pm)

This delightful tea, coffee and cake house in Primrose Hill provides a lovely spot to sit and watch the well-heeled crowd stroll by. Although small, the space is well utilised with a tantalising display of sweets and cakes, and an open frontage to make best use of the pavement tables. Laze away a Sunday afternoon with a coffee and a green tea chocolate gateau for something a little different.

OVERVIEW.

Catergory
Bakery Coffee Shop
Owner
Masayuki and Mina Hara
First Opened
2010

FOOD.

An intriguing combination of Japanese, French and British influences are evident in the breakfast, lunch and sweets menu

COFFEE & EQUIPMENT.

Coffee roaster
Monmouth Coffee Company
Coffee machine
Stafco G10, 2 groups
Coffee grinder
Mazzer Super Jolly

COFFEE PRICING.

Espresso	£1.65
Cappucino	£2.80
Latte	£2.80
Flat white	£2.80

CONTACT.

+44(0)20 7483 2544
www.lanka-uk.com
lanka@lanka-uk.com

RATING.

| COFFEE | 4.00 / 5 |
| OVERALL | 3.75 / 5 |

Look Mum No Hands!

49 Old Street, EC1V 9HX

This newcomer to the Shoreditch scene offers something innovative and lively. The owners' passion for cycling is clear for all to see – artfully decorating the interior are bicycles, parts, Tour de France memorabilia and framed jerseys. The layout is simple with high ceilings, wooden finishings and a bike workshop off to the side. The outdoor seating area offers a haven from bustling Old Street in which to enjoy a coffee, or an alcoholic drink from the licenced bar. A great destination with or without your bicycle.

OPEN.

Mon-Fri.	7:00am - 10:00pm
Sat.	9:00am - 10:00pm
Sun.	10:00am - 10:00pm

OVERVIEW.

Catergory
Retail & Leisure
Owner
Sam Humpheson, Matthew Harper and Lewin Chalkley
Head barista
Pepe Andzhej
First opened
2010

COFFEE & EQUIPMENT.

Coffee roaster
Square Mile Coffee Roasters
Coffee machine
Faema Due, 2 groups and La Marzocco Linea, 2 groups
Coffee grinder
Anfim

COFFEE PRICING.

Espresso	£1.50 / £1.80
Cappucino	£2.40
Latte	£2.40
Flat white	£2.10

FOOD.

Extensive menu for breakfast and lunch including bacon sarnies, muffins, crumpets, salads and pies. Tapas in the evenings. Plenty of vegetarian options

CONTACT.

+44(0)20 7253 1025
www.lookmumnohands.com
info@lookmumnohands.com

RATING.

COFFEE 4.00 / 5	🫘 🫘 🫘 🫘 🫘
OVERALL 4.25 / 5	★ ★ ★ ★ ⯪

Melrose and Morgan Primrose Hill

42 Gloucester Avenue, NW1 8JD ....

OPEN.

Mon-Fri.	8:00am - 7:00pm
Sat.	8:00am - 6:00pm
Sun.	9:00am - 5:00pm

This delightful grocer and deli is tucked away on a quiet street in leafy Primrose Hill. A constant stream of immaculately presented food is brought out from the open kitchen to the rustic wooden table in the centre of the store. If this is too tempting, perch by the window to watch the wandering passers-by as you enjoy your coffee.The grocer offers a mouth-watering selection of deli food, organic produce and ready-made meals to take home.

FOOD.

A tempting array of salads, quiches and pastries, plus cheese, chutney, ready meals and wine to take away

CONTACT.

+44(0)20 7722 0011
www.melroseandmorgan.com
info@melroseandmorgan.com

Sister coffee shops.
Hampstead

OVERVIEW.

Catergory
Eatery
Owner
Nick Selby and Ian James
First opened
2004

COFFEE & EQUIPMENT.

Coffee roaster
Monmouth Coffee Company
Coffee machine
La Marzocco Linea, 2 groups
Coffee grinder
Anfim

COFFEE PRICING.

Espresso	£1.40 / £1.60
Cappucino	£2.00
Latte	£2.00
Flat white	£2.00

RATING.

COFFEE		
4.25 / 5	🫘🫘🫘🫘🫘	
OVERALL		
3.75 / 5	★★★★☆	

Merito Coffee Stall Swiss Cottage Market

Eton Avenue, NW3 3EU ....

OPEN.
Wed, Fri. 8:30am - 5:00pm

Merito Coffee operate from the neighbourhood Swiss Cottage Market two days a week and the heaving Broadway Market on Saturdays. Merito use both an espresso machine and drip-filter on the simple premise of making good quality, unpretentious coffee. Regulars are greeted by name, and several varieties of coffee (beans or freshly ground) are available for purchase.

FOOD.

Home-made slices and biscuits are usually available

CONTACT.

+44(0)77 0312 1579
www.meritocoffee.com
jason@meritocoffee.com

Sister coffee shops.
Merito Coffee Stall
(Broadway Market)

OVERVIEW.

Catergory
Stall / Cart / Kiosk
Owner
Jason Fitzpatrick
Head barista
Ian Cameron
First Opened
2007

COFFEE & EQUIPMENT.

Coffee roaster
Coffee Plant espresso, filter coffee from various roasters
Coffee machine
Stafco, 2 groups
Coffee grinder
Anfim, Mazzer Super Jolly

COFFEE PRICING.

Espresso	£1.00 / £1.50
Cappucino	£1.80 / £2.00
Latte	£1.80 / £2.00
Flat white	£1.80

RATING.

COFFEE
4.50 / 5

Ottolenghi Islington

287 Upper Street, N1 2TZ

The food presentation here is nothing short of spectacular. Look through the window to the piles of beautiful meringues and fabulous cakes... now that they've drawn you inside, marvel at the colourful fresh salads and savouries on offer as you wait for a table (which you may well have to do on a weekend). Communal tables and a sleek modern design make the interior vibrant and social. The coffee here matches the quality of the food, creating an overall experience worth writing home about.

Sister coffee shops.
Notting Hill / Kensington / Belgravia

Images supplied by Ottolenghi

OPEN.

Mon-Sat.	8:00am - 11:00pm
Sun.	9:00am - 7:00pm

OVERVIEW.

Catergory
Eatery
Owner
Yotam Ottolenghi
Head barista
Chris Mok
First opened
2004

COFFEE & EQUIPMENT.

Coffee roaster
Square Mile Coffee Roasters
Coffee machine
La Marzocco Linea, 3 groups
Coffee grinder
Anfim

COFFEE PRICING.

Espresso	£1.50 / £2.30
Cappucino	£2.30
Latte	£2.30
Flat white	£2.30

FOOD.

Breakfast, lunch, dinner and everything in between, all freshly made on site and beautifully displayed

CONTACT.

+44(0)20 7288 1454
www.ottolenghi.co.uk
upper@ottolenghi.co.uk

RATING.

COFFEE
4.00 / 5

OVERALL
4.00 / 5

Pitch 42 @ Whitecross St. Market

Whitecross Street Market, EC1Y 8JL

OPEN.
Mon-Fri.   8:00am - 2:30pm

Pitch 42 at Whitecross Market has no signs or obvious branding - just look for the line of caffeine-hungry workers and you'll know you've found the right place. The coffee here is excellent. The baristas are experts in their trade and will skillfuly make your trusted favourite, or challenge you to try something new. Well worth going out of your way for.

Sister coffee shops.
Columbia Road Coffee Cart (Sundays)

OVERVIEW.

Catergory
Stall / Cart / Kiosk
Owner
Borough Olive Company
First Opened
2008

COFFEE & EQUIPMENT.

Coffee roaster
Square Mile Coffee Roasters
Coffee machine
La Marzocco Linea, 2 groups
Coffee grinder
Anfim, Mazzer Super Jolly

COFFEE PRICING.

Espresso	£1.00 / £1.50
Cappucino	£2.00
Latte	£2.00
Flat white	£2.00

RATING.

COFFEE
4.50 / 5

Sacred Highbury Studios
8 Hornsey Street, N7 8EG ....

OPEN.

Mon-Fri.	7:30am - 6:00pm
Sat.	9:00am - 5:00pm
Sun.	9:00am - 4:00pm

Located in the Highbury Studios complex amongst office buildings and close to London Metropolitan University, this spacious Sacred continues the New Zealand theme consistent across their cafés. There are plenty of comfy couches and quiet nooks to kick back and take time to enjoy your coffee. All of the Sacred food is produced in the large kitchen here.

FOOD.
Full breakfast, NZ-style brunch and lunch menu all cooked fresh on site

CONTACT.
+44(0)20 7700 1628
www.sacredcafe.co.uk
globalcoffee@gmail.com

Sister coffee shops.
Ganton Street / Covent Garden / Westfield / Kingly Court / Torrington Street

OVERVIEW.
Catergory
Chain
Owner
Tubbs Wanigasekera and Matt Clark
Head barista
Stephen Kenny
First opened
2009

COFFEE & EQUIPMENT.
Coffee roaster
Sacred House Roast
Coffee machine
La Marzocco Linea, 2 groups
Coffee grinder
Mazzer

COFFEE PRICING.

Espresso	£1.60
Cappucino	£2.50 / £2.70
Latte	£2.50 / £2.70
Flat white	£2.50 / £2.70

RATING.

COFFEE 4.25 / 5	🫘🫘🫘🫘🫘
OVERALL 4.00 / 5	★★★★★

Tina, We Salute You

47 King Henry's Walk, N1 4NH

Dalston locals are fiercely protective of Tina, We Salute You, a neighbourhood favourite since opening in 2009. The number of coffees chalked up on the brilliant loyalty wall proves just how much this café is loved. Every two months the interior is given over to a local artist to use as an exhibition space and do whatever they wish; this keeps things ever-changing and makes for a great talking point. Come and see this quirky gem for yourself.

OPEN.

Mon.	Closed
Tue.-Fri.	8:00am - 7:00pm
Sat.	9:00am - 7:00pm
Sun.	10:00am - 7:00pm

OVERVIEW.

Catergory
Artisanal Independent
Owner
Danny Hilton and Steve Hawkes
Head barista
Kerry Tyrrell, Lou Hartman and
Mana Elphickmoon
First opened
2009

COFFEE & EQUIPMENT.

Coffee roaster
Square Mile Coffee Roasters
Coffee machine
La Marzocco Linea, 3 groups
Coffee grinder
Anfim, Mazzer

COFFEE PRICING.

Espresso	£1.50 / £1.80
Cappucino	£2.20
Latte	£2.20
Flat white	£2.20

FOOD.

Choose from freshly-made bagels,
pastries, sandwiches and cakes,
or something off the morning
brunch menu.

CONTACT.

+44(0)20 3119 0047
www.tinawesaluteyou.com
tina@tinawesaluteyou.com

RATING.

COFFEE 4.50 / 5	🫘 🫘 🫘 🫘 🫘
OVERALL 4.50 / 5	★ ★ ★ ★ ⯪

Tinderbox

N1 Centre, Parkfield Street, N1 0PS

Image supplied by Tinderbox

OPEN.
Mon-Fri. 6:30am - 10:30pm

Deceptively small on the ground floor, Tinderbox has much more to offer than you may realise at first glance. The downstairs espresso bar is for takeaway only, so head up the wooden staircase to discover a large café with plenty of seating. Prized spots are the warm retro booths for a cosy chat over a Matthew Algie coffee, or the balcony seats to keep an eye on the passing crowd. Though not a particularly intimate venue, Tinderbox has considerable charm and character.

FOOD.

Sandwiches, snacks, cakes and treats for any time of day

CONTACT.

+44(0)20 7354 8929
tinderbox.upper@gmail.com

Sister coffee shops.
4 in Scotland / London Spitalfields (opening soon)

OVERVIEW.

Catergory
Chain
Owner
Carlo Ventisei
Head barista
Paula Bulgarerri
First opened
2009

COFFEE & EQUIPMENT.

Coffee roaster
Matthew Algie
Coffee machine
Electra Barlume, 3 groups
Coffee grinder
Mazzer

COFFEE PRICING.

Espresso	£1.55 / £1.95
Cappucino	£2.25 / £2.65
Latte	£1.85 / £2.25 / £2.65
Flat white	£2.25

RATING.

COFFEE 4.00 / 5	🫘 🫘 🫘 🫘 🫘
OVERALL 4.00 / 5	★ ★ ★ ★ ★

Wild and Wood Coffee

1-19 New Oxford Street, WC1A 1BA

Image supplied by Wild and Wood

OPEN.

Mon-Fri.	7:30am - 6:30pm
Sat.	9:00am - 6:00pm
Sun.	Closed

Wild and Wood is one of the oldest coffee shops in the area, open for over 30 years. The small interior has a warm and cosy feel, with wood panelling throughout, old church pew seats and an intimate seating 'nook'. Classic photographs and old school rock 'n' roll music add to the authentic charm of this delightful place. Monmouth coffee is served at some of the cheapest prices around.

FOOD.

An appetising array of pastries, sandwiches and cakes are nicely displayed by the window

CONTACT.

+44(0)75 2515 5957
wildwoodbean@yahoo.com

OVERVIEW.

Catergory
Artisanal Independent
Owner / head barista
Bozena Mazerant
First Opened
1978

COFFEE & EQUIPMENT.

Coffee roaster
Monmouth Coffee Company
Coffee machine
La Spaziale, 2 groups
Coffee grinder
Mazzer Luigi

COFFEE PRICING.

Espresso	£1.00 / £1.30
Cappucino	£1.90
Latte	£1.90
Flat white	£1.90

Also serve
**single origin
filter coffee**

RATING.

COFFEE 4.00 / 5	🫘 🫘 🫘 🫘 🫘
OVERALL 3.75 / 5	★ ★ ★ ★ ★

TRUE ARTISANS.

La Marzocco

Inner East

London's Inner East is undergoing a huge revival associated with an explosion of restaurants, cafés and bars in the area. Lively and culturally captivating, it is sure to produce many more new and inventive coffee shops in the coming years.

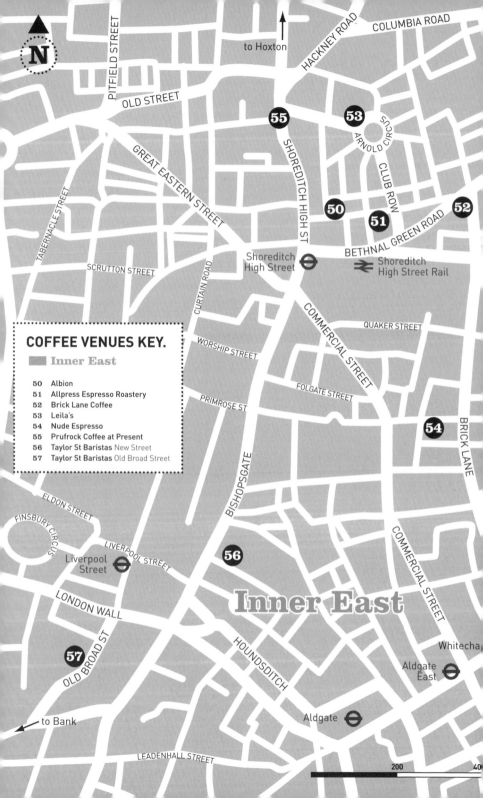

N

PITFIELD STREET

COLUMBIA ROAD

HACKNEY ROAD

to Hoxton

OLD STREET

GREAT EASTERN STREET

TABERNACLE STREET

SCRUTTON STREET

SHOREDITCH HIGH ST

ARNOLD CIRCUS

CLUB ROW

BETHNAL GREEN ROAD

55

53

50

51

52

Shoreditch
High Street

Shoreditch
High Street Rail

CURTAIN ROAD

WORSHIP STREET

COMMERCIAL STREET

QUAKER STREET

FOLGATE STREET

PRIMROSE ST

COFFEE VENUES KEY.

Inner East

50 Albion
51 Allpress Espresso Roastery
52 Brick Lane Coffee
53 Leila's
54 Nude Espresso
55 Prufrock Coffee at Present
56 Taylor St Baristas New Street
57 Taylor St Baristas Old Broad Street

BISHOPSGATE

BRICK LANE

54

ELDON STREET

FINSBURY CIRCUS

LIVERPOOL STREET

Liverpool
Street

LONDON WALL

OLD BROAD ST

56

57

COMMERCIAL STREET

Inner East

HOUNDSDITCH

Whitecha

Aldgate
East

to Bank

Aldgate

LEADENHALL STREET

200   40

Albion

2-4 Boundary Street, E2 7DD

Image supplied by Albion

OPEN.
Mon-Sun. 8:00am - 12:00am

Albion is a spacious and welcoming venue in the heart of Shoreditch. The atmosphere is vibrant and upbeat as customers gathered for business meetings, family occasions and social catch-ups happily share the dining area. Large glass concertina doors permit lots of natural light and extend the space onto the pavement on sunny days. Enjoy your coffee with a proudly British, locally sourced meal or treat from the open kitchen and bakery.

FOOD.

British caff food - hearty breakfasts, pies, sandwiches and fish and chips. Takeaways and fresh produce are available from the grocer at the entrance

CONTACT.

+44(0)20 7729 1051
www.albioncaff.co.uk
info@theboundary.co.uk

OVERVIEW.

Catergory
Eatery
Owner
Sir Terence Conran, Vicki Conran and Peter Prescott
First opened
2009

COFFEE & EQUIPMENT.

Coffee roaster
L'Unico
Coffee machine
Gaggia E50 Evolution, 2 groups
Coffee grinder
Mazzer Super Jolly

COFFEE PRICING.

Espresso	£2.00 / £2.50
Cappucino	£2.60
Latte	£2.60
Flat white	£2.60

RATING.

COFFEE
3.75 / 5

OVERALL
3.75 / 5

Allpress Espresso Roastery

58 Redchurch Street, E2 7DJ ·····································

The highly anticipated first UK venture for well-established New Zealand-based roastery Allpress Espresso has just opened in the heart of Shoreditch. The simple, natural interior keeps the focus on the coffee itself, with a gleaming roaster on proud display and coffee expertise evident in every detail of this space. Allpress have had huge success in New Zealand and Australia, supplying many coffee shops and high-end restaurants on both sides of the Tasman. This quality new venture will throw out a challenge to the UK market, for London coffee lovers to follow with keen interest.

Image supplied by Allpress Espresso Roastery

TOP 30

OPEN.

Tue-Fri. 7:30am - 4:30pm
Sat-Sun. 9:00am - 5:00pm

OVERVIEW.

Catergory
Artisanal Independent
Owner
Michael Allpress and Tony Papas
First opened
2010

COFFEE & EQUIPMENT.

Coffee roaster
Allpress
Coffee machine
La Marzocco Linea, 3 groups
Coffee grinder
Mazzer Robur, Mazzer Super Jolly, Mahlkönig

COFFEE PRICING.

Espresso	£2.50
Cappucino	£2.50
Latte	£2.50
Flat white	£2.50

FOOD.

A selection of creative Italian sandwiches, pastries and light dishes

CONTACT.

+44(0)20 7749 1780
www.allpressespresso.com
coffee@allpress.co.uk

The **Marco Über Boiler** is designed to deliver exact volumes of hot water at precise temperatures. Roasting is done on site

RATING.

COFFEE 4.50 / 5	🌰 🌰 🌰 🌰 🌰
OVERALL 4.50 / 5	★ ★ ★ ★ ⯪

Brick Lane Coffee

157 Brick Lane, E1 6SB

Situated at the northern end of Brick Lane, this coffee shop oozes alternative cool. Unashamedly punk, the mish-mash of furniture, eclectic decor and bicycles crammed inside combine to create a share-house, retro feel. The crowd of artsy East Londoners linger on the couches as rock music plays in the background. If you're not in the mood for a coffee, the smoothies and frappes are also a popular choice.

OPEN.
Mon-Fri. 7:00am - 8:00pm
Sat-Sun. 8:00am - 7:00pm

OVERVIEW.
Catergory
Chain
Owner
Street Coffee / Adrian Jones
First opened
2001

COFFEE & EQUIPMENT.
Coffee roaster
Ethica Coffee
Coffee machine
Rancilio Classe 8, 3 groups
Coffee grinder
Mazzer Super Jolly, Mazzer Mini

Sister coffee shops.
Goswell Road / Bermondsey Street

COFFEE PRICING.

Espresso	£1.70 / £1.50
Cappucino	£2.00 / £2.35 / £2.70
Latte	£2.00 / £2.35 / £2.70
Flat white	£2.00 / £2.35 / £2.70

FOOD.
A selection of sandwiches, soups and snacks

CONTACT.
+44(0)20 7729 2667

RATING.

| COFFEE 4.25 / 5 |
| OVERALL 4.25 / 5 |

Leila's
17 Calvert Avenue, E2 7JP

A pleasant, unassuming café in a quiet corner of Shoreditch, Leila's offers an oasis of calm. The place has a rustic feel, as though you have stepped into someone's country house. The open-plan kitchen combines well with the wooden finishings and light, neutral walls to create a cosy environment. A great place to go to wind down, read a book or take some time out to catch up with an old friend.

OPEN.

Mon-Tue. Closed
Wed-Sat. 10:00am - 6:00pm
Sun. 10:00am - 5:00pm

OVERVIEW.

Catergory
Artisanal Independent
Owner
Leila McAlister
Head barista
Jack Coleman
First opened
2002

COFFEE & EQUIPMENT.

Coffee roaster
Monmouth Coffee Company
Coffee machine
La Marzocco Linea, 2 groups
Coffee grinder
Mazzer Super Jolly

COFFEE PRICING.

Espresso £1.50
Cappucino £2.00 / £2.40
Latte £2.00 / £2.40
Flat white £2.00

FOOD.

A small daily-changing menu
of soups, sandwiches and
home-made treats

CONTACT.

+44(0)20 7729 9789
info@leilasshop.com

RATING.

COFFEE 4.00 / 5
OVERALL 4.00 / 5

Nude Espresso

26 Hanbury Street, E1 6QR

Located close to the bustling Spitalfields market, Nude Espresso offers much more than just a caffeine hit to those looking to escape the crowds. The clean lines and design of the café make it a cosy space to recuperate, recharge and catch up on the latest. Nude roast their own signature East espresso blend, which is brought to life by well-trained baristas. Often jam-packed on weekends - you have been warned!

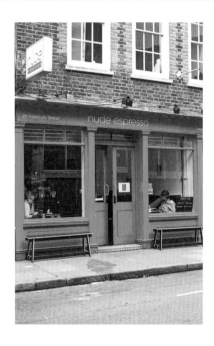

COFFEE PRICING.

Espresso	£2.00
Cappucino	£2.50 / £3.00
Latte	£2.50 / £3.00
Flat white	£2.50 / £3.00

FOOD.

An appetising Antipodean-style breakfast and brunch menu and tempting display of baked goods.

CONTACT.

+44(0)78 0422 3590
www.nudeespresso.com
rich@nudeespresso.com

OPEN.

Mon-Fri. 7:30am - 6:00pm
Sat-Sun. 10:00am - 6:00pm

OVERVIEW.

Catergory
Artisanal Independent
Owner
Richard Reed
Head barista
Sasha McGinley
First opened
2008

COFFEE & EQUIPMENT.

Coffee roaster
Nude Espresso
Coffee machine
Wega, 3 groups
Coffee grinder
Compak K10

Sister coffee shops.
Nude Espresso Roastery

RATING.

COFFEE
4.75 / 5

OVERALL
4.50 / 5

Prufrock Coffee at Present

140 Shoreditch High Street, E1 6JE

OPEN.

Mon-Fri.	10:30am - 6:00pm
Sat.	11:00am - 5:00pm
Sun.	12:00pm - 4:00pm

Located inside über-cool men's clothing store Present on Shoreditch High Street, Prufrock makes for a fascinating visit. Watch and learn from the experts as Gwilym and Matthias experiment in their quest to pull the perfect coffee, using fully manual equipment. A free coffee here is the prize for completing Gwilym's Disloyalty card.

COFFEE PRICING.

Espresso	£1.50
Cappucino	£2.40
Latte	£2.40
Flat white	£2.20

CONTACT.

www.prufrockcoffee.com
info@prufrockcoffee.com

OVERVIEW.

Catergory
Stall / Cart / Kiosk
Owner
Gwilym Davies and
Jeremy Challender
Head barista
Mattias Björklund
First opened
2009

COFFEE & EQUIPMENT.

Coffee roaster
Square Mile Coffee Roasters
Coffee machine
La Victoria Arduino, 2 groups, modified
Coffee grinder
Anfim, Mazzer Robur E, modified

RATING.

COFFEE
4.75 / 5

Taylor St Baristas New Street

1A New Street, EC2M 4TP ....

OPEN.

Mon-Fri.	7:00am - 5:00pm
Sat.	Closed
Sun.	10:00am - 4:00pm

Australian siblings Nick, Andrew and Laura Tolley opened this coffee shop in the summer of 2008 and have since developed a reputation as one of the leaders of the third wave coffee scene. Their tiny New St location attracts a steady stream of city suits and Spitalfields shoppers at any time of day for good reason. Taylor St pride themselves on employing experienced baristas and their catch phrase of 'Finely crafted coffee for serious coffee drinkers' rings true.

FOOD.

An appetising spread of bakery goods, sandwiches and salads are prepared on site daily

CONTACT.

+44(0)20 7929 2207
www.taylor-st.com
info@taylor-st.com

Sister coffee shops.

Old Broad Street / Richmond / Shoreditch / Brighton

OVERVIEW.

Catergory
Chain
Owner
Nick, Andrew and Laura Tolley
Head barista
Andrew Tolley
First Opened
2008

COFFEE & EQUIPMENT.

Coffee roaster
Union Hand-Roasted
Coffee machine
Nuevo Simmonelli Aurelia, 3 groups
Coffee grinder
Anfim Super Caimano x 2, Mazzer Super Jolly

COFFEE PRICING.

Espresso	£1.20 / £1.40
Cappucino	£2.20 / £2.40 / £2.95
Latte	£2.20 / £2.40 / £2.95
Flat white	£2.20

RATING.

COFFEE 4.50 / 5

OVERALL 4.00 / 5

Taylor St Baristas Old Broad Street
125 Old Broad Street, EC2N 1AR

The newest venture for the Taylor St family is a much larger, more spacious affair than their New St location. The design is very sleek with lofty high ceilings, timber finishings and funky drop lights, and the daily menu is projected onto the wall behind the bar. A great place for a business meeting or lunchtime escape from the pressures of a working day in the city.

Sister coffee shops.
New Street / Richmond / Shoreditch / Brighton

OPEN.
Mon-Fri. 7:30am - 5:00pm
Sat-Sun. Closed

OVERVIEW.
Catergory
Chain
Owner
Nick, Andrew and Laura Tolley
Head barista
Andrew Tolley
First opened
2010

COFFEE & EQUIPMENT.
Coffee roaster
Union Hand-Roasted
Coffee machine
Nuevo Simmonelli Aurelia, 3 groups
and Synesso Hydra, 3 groups
Coffee grinder
Anfim Super Caimano,
Mazzer Robur E

COFFEE PRICING.

Espresso	£1.20 / £1.40
Cappucino	£2.20 / £2.40 / £2.95
Latte	£2.20 / £2.40 / £2.95
Flat white	£2.20

FOOD.
Delicious fresh salads, sandwiches,
soups and more made on site daily

CONTACT.
+44(0)79 8158 9484
www.taylor-st.com
info@taylor-st.com

RATING.

COFFEE 4.50 / 5

OVERALL 4.50 / 5

Hackney

Hackney has successfully shaken
its label as a rough outer region
to emerge as London's booming
artistic neighbourhood. A wonderful
combination of cultures and a thriving
creative scene have helped put
Hackney back on the map. The world's
attention will be on the area during
the 2012 Olympics, providing an
excellent opportunity for new coffee
venues to make their mark.

Cà Phê VN (Saigon Street Cafe)

Broadway Market, E8 4PH ....

If you like your coffee strong and different, this is the place for you. Occupying a corner stall of Hackney's Broadway Market every Saturday, Cá Phé VN provides a Vietnamese-style caffeine hit like no other in London. Relax in a canvas deck chair and enjoy a heart-starting iced coffee (their summer specialty) as the eclectic market crowd stroll by. Husband and wife Rob Atthill and Tuyen Hong source their coffee directly from farmers in Vietnam and also sell wholesale to numerous suppliers and restaurants across the UK.

OPEN.

Sat.   10:00am - 5:00pm

OVERVIEW.

Catergory
Stall / Cart / Kiosk
Owner
Rob Atthill and Tuyen Hong
Head barista
Khoa Nguyen
First opened
2007

COFFEE & EQUIPMENT.

Coffee roaster
Cà Phê VN
Coffee machine
Drip filter

Sister coffee shops.
Café VN Clerkenwell Road /
Caphe House Bermondsey

Also serve
**Vietnamese
iced coffee -**
£2.00

COFFEE PRICING.

All coffees £1.50 - Vietnamese
specialties, either black or
sweetened with condensed milk

FOOD.

Try Cá Phé VN's celebrated five pork
baguette, their version of typical
Vietnamese street food

CONTACT.

+44(0)77 8078 4696
www.caphevn.co.uk
caphevn@aol.com

RATING.

COFFEE 4.25 / 5	🫘 🫘 🫘 🫘 🫘

Climpson & Sons

67 Broadway Market, E8 4PH ....

Revered by coffee lovers in East London, Climpson & Sons has developed an incredibly loyal following since opening in 2004. Their roastery is located just up the road and a variety of blends are available for purchase here at the café. On a Saturday you would be lucky to even make it through the door whilst the Broadway Market is in full swing – luckily the same team operate a stall at the southern end of the market to help meet demand.

OPEN.

Mon-Fri. 8:00am - 5:00pm
Sat. 8:30am - 5:00pm
Sun. 9:00am - 4:00pm

OVERVIEW.

Catergory
Artisanal Independent
Owner
Ian Burgess
Head barista
Danny Davies
First opened
2004

COFFEE & EQUIPMENT.

Coffee roaster
Climpson & Sons
Coffee machine
La Marzocco Linea, 3 groups
Coffee grinder
Mazzer

Sister coffee shops.
Climpson & Sons Broadway
Market Stall

COFFEE PRICING.

Espresso	£1.40 / £1.70
Cappucino	£2.00
Latte	£2.00
Flat white	£2.00

FOOD.

Fresh sandwiches and grilled toasts
are made with produce sourced from
local businesses

CONTACT.

+44(0)20 7812 9829
www.webcoffeeshop.co.uk

Climpson & Sons **roast their own
beans** at their roastery
just up the road

RATING.

COFFEE
4.75 / 5

OVERALL
4.50 / 5

Columbia Road Coffee Cart

Off Ezra Street, Columbia Road Flower Market, E2 7RH

OPEN.

Sun. 8:00am - 2:00pm

This coffee cart, tucked away in a courtyard off Ezra Street, does a roaring trade every Sunday during the Columbia Road Flower Market. Awarded baristas come up with the goods every time, using the gleaming espresso machine from the world barista championships. There's good reason why there is usually a queue for much of the day.

COFFEE PRICING.

Espresso	£1.00
Cappucino	£2.20
Latte	£2.20
Flat white	£2.20

CONTACT.

info@prufrockcoffee.com

OVERVIEW.

Catergory
Stall / Cart / Kiosk
Owner
Borough Olive Company
Head barista
Lee Harte
First opened
2005

COFFEE & EQUIPMENT.

Coffee roaster
Square Mile Coffee Roasters
Coffee machine
Nuevo Simonelli, 3 groups
Coffee grinder
Anfim

Sister coffee shops.
Pitch 42 @ Whitecross Market

RATING.

COFFEE 4.75 / 5

The Container Café

View Tube, Stratford, E15 2PJ ....

OPEN.

Mon-Fri.	9:00am - 5:00pm
Sat-Sun.	10:00am - 6:00pm

The Container Café is located at the heart of the London Olympic site, in the unmissable View Tube building. The café is unpretentious and laid back, with a communal table, retro furniture and comfortable lounge seats. The large windows and several outdoor tables provide the perfect vantage point to watch the stadium grow before your eyes and imagine how it will look by 2012. Great coffee and scrumptious food are consistent with sister café The Counter, located a short walk away.

FOOD.

Freshly made breakfast, bagels, soups and sandwiches. Try the delicious bacon baguette with home-made relish

CONTACT.

+44(0)78 3427 5687
www.theviewtube.co.uk
info@thecountercafe.co.uk

Sister coffee shops.
The Counter Café

OVERVIEW.

Catergory
Artisanal Independent
Owner
Tom and Jess Seaton
Head barista
Paul Banks
First Opened
2009

COFFEE & EQUIPMENT.

Coffee roaster
Square Mile Coffee Roasters
Coffee machine
La Marzocco Linea, 2 groups
Coffee grinder
Anfim

COFFEE PRICING.

Espresso	£1.40
Cappucino	£2.00
Latte	£2.50
Flat white	£2.00

RATING.

COFFEE	4.25 / 5
OVERALL	4.25 / 5

101

The Counter Café

4a Roach Road, E3 2PA

OPEN.

Mon-Fri. 7:30am-5:00pm
Sat-Sun. 9:00am-5:00pm

(Summer: Open til 10:00pm
Thurs-Sat for tapas)

The Counter is a truly unique café bursting with character. Improbably located amongst workshops and warehouses in the heart of Hackney, the set-up here is brilliant. Exposed brick, colourful feature walls and bare floors combine to create an unfinished but cosy feel. The blue retro flip-up theatre seats are a great touch. Outside, get comfy on the sofa and check out the backyard street art (or spot the Tom Selleck propaganda!). Coffee is excellent, service welcoming and the breakfast mouth-watering. A must-see.

FOOD.

Comprehensive breakfast menu, baguettes, bagels and sweet treats

CONTACT.

+44(0)78 3427 5920
www.thecountercafe.co.uk
info@thecountercafe.co.uk

Sister coffee shops.
The Container Café

OVERVIEW.

Catergory
Artisanal Independent
Owner
Tom and Jess Seaton
Head barista
Fletcher Barns
First opened
2009

COFFEE & EQUIPMENT.

Coffee roaster
Square Mile Coffee Roasters
Coffee machine
La Marzocco Linea, 2 groups
Coffee grinder
Anfim

COFFEE PRICING.

Espresso	£1.40
Cappucino	£2.00
Latte	£2.50
Flat white	£2.00

RATING.

COFFEE 4.25 / 5

OVERALL 4.50 / 5

The Hackney Pearl

11 Prince Edward Road, E9 5LX

OPEN.
Mon-Sun. 10:00am - 11:00pm

The Hackney Pearl is an artsy, stylish venue located in the middle of an industrial area. The shopfront is largely glass, allowing in lots of natural light so customers can watch the streetside happenings from the comfort of indoors. The menu changes daily and there is an extensive bar list in case coffee isn't quite enough for you. Open til late every evening.

FOOD.

Panini, soups, salads, cakes and a rotating a la carte menu

CONTACT.

+44(0)20 8510 3605
www.thehackneypearl.com
info@thehackneypearl.com

OVERVIEW.

Catergory
Artisanal Independent
Owner
James Morgan
First opened
2009

COFFEE & EQUIPMENT.

Coffee roaster
Square Mile Coffee Roasters
Coffee machine
Gaggia D90, 3 groups
Coffee grinder
Mazzer Super Jolly

COFFEE PRICING.

Espresso	£1.60 / £2.00
Cappucino	£2.00
Latte	£2.00
Flat white	£2.00

RATING.

COFFEE 4.00 / 5	🫘 🫘 🫘 🫘 🫘
OVERALL 3.75 / 5	★ ★ ★ ★ ★

Hurwundeki Café

298 Cambridge Heath Road, E2 9HA ....

OPEN.

Mon-Fri. 7:00am - 6:00pm
Sat-Sun. 9:00am - 6:00pm

Hurwundeki is one of many new cafés to have popped up in Hackney, but it succeeds in standing out from the crowd. Vintage is the theme here – the rustic interior has an unfinished look, with lovely unpolished floorboards and antique furniture (also for sale). Outdoor courtyard seating overlooks a sand-covered play area for the little ones. The same owner runs a hair salon and vintage boutique clothing store, both nearby.

FOOD.

Muesli, pastries, an assortment of salads, sandwiches, 'croissandwiches' and quiche. Mostly organic food with plenty of vegetarian choices

CONTACT.

+44(0)20 7749 0638
www.hurwundeki.com
info@hurwundeki.com

OVERVIEW.

Catergory
Artisanal Independent
Owner
Ki-Chul Lee
Head barista
Pawel Grygo
First Opened
2009

COFFEE & EQUIPMENT.

Coffee roaster
Square Mile Coffee Roasters
Coffee machine
La Marzocco Linea, 2 groups
Coffee grinder
Mazzer

COFFEE PRICING.

Espresso   £1.70 / £1.95
Cappucino   £1.90
Latte   £1.90
Flat white £1.90

RATING.

| COFFEE 4.00 / 5 | 🫘 🫘 🫘 🫘 🫘 |
| OVERALL 3.75 / 5 | ★ ★ ★ ★ ★ |

Lemon Monkey

188 Stoke Newington High Street, N16 7JD ....

OPEN.

Mon-Sat.   9:00am - 6:00pm
Sun.   10:00am - 6:00pm

Open late some Fridays

Lemon Monkey is a cheerful, family-friendly Stoke Newington local. Offering Mozzo coffee alongside a continental-style menu, it is a welcoming and unassuming café with a real community feel. Inside is much larger than it appears from the street, and offers plenty of seating as well as shelves stocked full of produce, chutneys and wine to take home. Open late some Friday evenings for events and live music.

FOOD.

Continental breakfast, salads, quiche, specialty cheeses and shared platters. Special children's menu

CONTACT.

+44(0)20 7241 4454
www.lemon-monkey.co.uk
lemon.monkey@btconnect.com

OVERVIEW.

Catergory
Artisanal Independent
Owner
Katharine Tasker
First Opened
2007

COFFEE & EQUIPMENT.

Coffee roaster
Mozzo
Coffee machine
La Marzocco Linea, 2 groups
Coffee grinder
Mazzer Luigi

COFFEE PRICING.

Espresso	£1.50
Cappucino	£2.50
Latte	£2.50
Flat white	£2.25

RATING.

COFFEE
4.00 / 5

OVERALL
4.00 / 5

105

Merito Coffee Stall Broadway Mkt.

Broadway Market, E8 4PH ....

OPEN.
Sat. 9:00am - 5:00pm

Merito Coffee operate from the neighbourhood Swiss Cottage Market two days a week and the heaving Broadway Market on Saturdays. Merito use both an espresso machine and drip-filter on the simple premise of making good quality, unpretentious coffee. Regulars are greeted by name, and several varieties of coffee (beans or freshly ground) are available for purchase.

FOOD.
Home-made slices and biscuits are usually available

CONTACT.
+44(0)77 0312 1579
www.meritocoffee.com
jason@meritocoffee.com

Sister coffee shops.
Swiss Cottage Market

OVERVIEW.
Catergory
Stall / Cart / Kiosk
Owner
Jason Fitzpatrick
Head barista
Ian Cameron
First Opened
2007

COFFEE & EQUIPMENT.
Coffee roaster
Coffee Plant espresso, filter coffee from various roasters
Coffee machine
Stafco, 2 groups
Coffee grinder
Anfim, Mazzer Super Jolly

COFFEE PRICING.
Espresso £1.00 / £1.50
Cappucino £1.80 / £2.00
Latte £1.80 / £2.00
Flat white £1.80

RATING.

COFFEE 4.50 / 5

Pavilion

Corner Old Ford Road & Grove Rd, Victoria Park, E9 7DE ....

OPEN.
Mon-Sun. 8:30am - 4:00pm

Perfectly positioned overlooking the lake in beautiful Victoria Park, Pavilion offers excellent coffee to an everyday café crowd. The emphasis on quality extends to the food menu, which is made up of local ingredients sourced from Borough Market. Come here for brunch on a sunny weekend to see Pavilion at its best – arrive early to avoid the queue.

FOOD.

Cooked breakfasts, daily lunch menu, sandwiches, baked treats and cakes

CONTACT.

+44(0)20 8980 0030
www.the-pavilion-cafe.com

Sister coffee shops.
Elliots (Redchurch Street)

OVERVIEW.

Catergory
Artisanal Independent
Owner
Brett Redman and Rob Green
First Opened
2007

COFFEE & EQUIPMENT.

Coffee roaster
Square Mile Coffee Roasters
Coffee machine
Synesso Cyncra, 3 groups
Coffee grinder
Anfim

COFFEE PRICING.

Espresso	£1.50
Cappucino	£2.20
Latte	£2.20
Flat white	£2.20

RATING.

COFFEE 4.00 / 5	
OVERALL 4.00 / 5	

Taste of Bitter Love

276 Hackney Road, E2 7SJ ··

Taste of Bitter Love is a tiny café on hectic Hackney Road. This quirky coffee shop with its ramshackle antique wooden chairs spilling onto the pavement oozes personality, and is well-respected by locals and coffee-lovers in the know. Coffee is expertly made by friendly baristas and the food is delicious. This place has all the ingredients of a favourite local haunt, but is well worth crossing town for.

OPEN.

Mon-Fri.	7:30am - 4:00pm
Sat-Sun.	10:00am - 3:30pm

OVERVIEW.

Catergory
Artisanal Independent
Owner / head barista
Felicity Whitehead and Bill Tahtis
First opened
2008

COFFEE & EQUIPMENT.

Coffee roaster
Square Mile Coffee Roasters
Coffee machine
La Marzocco Linea, 2 groups
Coffee grinder
Anfim x 2, Santos

COFFEE PRICING.

Espresso	£1.50 / £1.80
Cappucino	£2.00
Latte	£1.90
Flat white	£2.00

FOOD.

Freshly made baguettes, salads,
muffins and wholesome cakes

CONTACT.

www.tasteofbitterlove.com
info@tasteofbitterlove.com

RATING.

COFFEE 4.50 / 5	🫘🫘🫘🫘🫘
OVERALL 4.25 / 5	★★★★⯪

Towpath
42 De Beauvoir Crescent, N1 5SB

Towpath is a well-hidden café tucked alongside the canal in Hackney. It is a relaxed and modest venue serving Italian coffee and a selection of homemade meals and snacks. Alfresco tables provide fantastic spots to watch the constant stream of runners pounding the canal-side pavement. The communal table under cover adds to the family-friendly and neighbourly feel of this lovely place.

Images supplied by Towpath

OPEN.

Tue-Fri.	8:00am - 5:00pm
Sat.	9:00am - 5:00pm
Sun.	10:00am - 5:00pm

OVERVIEW.

Catergory
Artisanal Independent
Owner
Jason Lowe and Lori de Mori
Head barista
Amanda Thompson
First Opened
2010

COFFEE & EQUIPMENT.

Coffee roaster
Piansa
Coffee machine
La Marzocco Linea manual, 2 goups
Coffee grinder
Eureka Conti Valerio

COFFEE PRICING.

Espresso	£1.30
Cappucino	£2.00
Latte	£2.00

FOOD.

Choose from breakfast, quiche,
savoury tarts, cakes and
daily specials

CONTACT.

+44(0)20 7254 7606

RATING.

COFFEE 3.75 / 5	🫘 🫘 🫘 🫘 🫘
OVERALL 3.75 / 5	★ ★ ★ ★ ★

111

Wilton Way Café

63 Wilton Way, E8 1BG ··

Wilton Way Café straddles the line between art space and coffee shop remarkably well. Open in its current form since late 2009, the café incorporates a radio space for live local broadcasts, as well as rotating art exhibits. With its unique bar design and funky retro lampshades, Wilton Way Café attracts a varied crowd of people looking for a place to relax, enjoy a fine cup of coffee and perhaps be entertained or inspired.

Hackney

OPEN.

Mon-Sat.	8:00am - 5:00pm
Sun.	9:00am - 5:00pm

OVERVIEW.

Catergory
Artisanal Independent
Owner
David McHugh
Head barista
Peter Willes
First opened
2009

COFFEE & EQUIPMENT.

Coffee roaster
Climpson & Sons
Coffee machine
La Marzocco Linea, 2 groups
Coffee grinder
Mazzer Super Jolly

COFFEE PRICING.

Espresso	£1.00 / £1.70
Cappucino	£2.00 / £2.20
Latte	£2.00 / £2.20
Flat white	£2.00 / £2.20

FOOD.

The all-day brunch menu includes sourdough toasts and bacon baps; or try sandwiches and pastries for lunch

CONTACT.

+44(0)20 7249 0444
www.londonfieldsradio.com
dom@londonfieldsradio.com

RATING.

| COFFEE 4.50 / 5 | 🫘 🫘 🫘 🫘 🫘 |
| OVERALL 4.50 / 5 | ★ ★ ★ ★ ✬ |

South East London

London's fascinating South East combines iconic tourist attractions around London Bridge and Greenwich with the up-and-coming edginess of Deptford and Brockley. From upmarket dining experiences to unique hidden cafés, this area has it all.

Brown's of Brockley

5 Coulgate Street, SE4 2RW

OPEN.

Mon-Fri.	7:00am - 5:00pm
Sat.	9:00am - 5:00pm
Sun.	9:00am - 12:00pm

A stylish café and deli opposite the Brockley train station, Brown's has rapidly developed a reputation as one of the only places to go for a good coffee in the area. With its simple layout and natural colour scheme, Brown's is a cosy and relaxing place to step in and slow down. Bookshelves house record collections, books to peruse and the odd board game to play with fellow caffeine hunters at the communal table. Beautiful photography decorating the walls is for sale.

FOOD.

A selection of fresh deli-style foods including croissants, pastries, cakes and sandwiches

CONTACT.

+44(0)20 8692 0722
ross@brownsofbrockley.com

OVERVIEW.

Catergory
Artisanal Independent
Owner / Head barista
Ross Brown
First opened
2009

COFFEE & EQUIPMENT.

Coffee roaster
Square Mile Coffee Roasters
Coffee machine
La Marzocco FB70, 2 groups
Coffee grinder
Anfim (modified)

COFFEE PRICING.

Espresso	£1.00
Cappucino	£2.00
Latte	£2.00
Flat white	£2.00

RATING.

COFFEE	4.25 / 5
OVERALL	4.25 / 5

Del'Aziz Bankside
5 Canvey Street, SE1 9AN ···

OPEN.
Mon-Sun. 8:00am - 11:00pm

Del'Aziz successfully combines a café, restaurant, deli and bakery to create one vibrant and colourful venue on the south bank of the River Thames. Influences range from the Mediterranean to Northern Africa via the Middle East. The restaurant interior is fun and bright, the atmosphere warm and convivial. Great for a coffee break during your working day or an enjoyable evening outing.

FOOD.

An irresistable selection of bakery products, gourmet sandwiches, fresh salads and Eastern Mediterranean specialties

CONTACT.

+44(0)20 7633 0033
www.delaziz.co.uk
bankside@delaziz.co.uk

Sister coffee shops.
Bermondsey / Fulham / Swiss Cottage / Westfield

OVERVIEW.

Catergory
Eatery
Owner
Shahroka and Zehra Parvin
First opened
2003

COFFEE & EQUIPMENT.

Coffee roaster
Molinari
Coffee machine
Wega Vela, 4 groups
Coffee grinder
Mazzer Super Jolly

COFFEE PRICING.

Espresso	£1.50 / £1.80
Cappucino	£1.80 / £2.20 / £2.50
Latte	£1.80 / £2.20 / £2.50
Flat white	£1.80 / £2.20 / £2.50

RATING.

COFFEE 4.00 / 5

OVERALL 4.00 / 5

The Deptford Project
121-123 Deptford High Street, SE8 4NS ·····································

The Deptford Project is an innovative café in the shell of a decomissioned 1960's train carriage in an up-and-coming area of London. Delightfully quirky, it is worth a visit for interest's sake alone. Colourful, often-changing street art covers the train exterior. The outside decking provides the perfect spot to soak up some sunshine on warm days, while inside is light-filled and communal. A creative hub for the artistic, the curious or the just plain hungry to enjoy lunch and a Darlington's coffee.

OPEN.
Mon-Sat. 9:00am - 6:00pm
Sun. 9:00am - 5:00pm

OVERVIEW.
Catergory
Artisanal Independent
Owner
Rebecca Molina
Head barista
JP Martin Zamora
First Opened
2008

COFFEE & EQUIPMENT.
Coffee roaster
Darlington's
Coffee machine
La Marzocco, 2 groups
Coffee grinder
Espresso Italiano

COFFEE PRICING.
Espresso   £1.30 / £1.90
Cappucino £1.90
Latte   £1.90
Flat white £1.80

FOOD.
Fresh organic quiches, salads and baked potatoes are prepared on site

CONTACT.
+44(0)75 4559 3279
www.thedeptfordproject.com
rebecca@thedeptfordproject.com

RATING.

COFFEE
3.75 / 5

OVERALL
3.75 / 5

Exchange Coffee
Lewisham Market, Lee High Road end (next to the clock tower)

Exchange Coffee, a stall at the Saturday Lewisham Market, has a lovely neighbourly vibe. A steady stream of customers is greeted with a warm smile and friendly conversation. Coffee is poured with precision, just the right amount of milk and finished off with award-winning latte art. Owner Neil experiments with several different coffee roasters and has also started roasting on site.

Sister coffee shops.
Also service events and festivals

SE13 6BB ....

Images supplied by Exchange Coffee

Sat. 8:00am - 5:00pm

OVERVIEW.

Catergory
Stall / Cart / Kiosk
Owner
Neil Le Bihan
Head barista
Chris Whitelaw
First opened
2009

COFFEE & EQUIPMENT.

Coffee roaster
Monmouth Coffee Company, Caravan
Coffee machine
La Marzocco Linea, 2 groups
Coffee grinder
Mazzer Robur E, Anfim

Also serve
filter coffee
& occasionally
roast on site

COFFEE PRICING.

Espresso	£1.00
Cappucino	£2.00
Latte	£2.00
Flat white	£2.00

FOOD.

Try a slice of home-made cake or
bread and jam, free with your coffee

CONTACT.

+44(0)78 1159 2024
neil.lebihan@yahoo.com

RATING.

COFFEE
4.75 / 5

Monmouth Coffee Company
2 Park Street, SE1 9AB

Monmouth Coffee Company has developed a cult-like following among many Londoners who claim they will never again drink any other coffee. The Borough site, larger than Covent Garden, is incredibly popular, as people flock to taste the hallowed liquid gold for themselves. Fridays and Saturdays are extremely busy, so to fully immerse yourself in the Monmouth experience a weekday visit might be a safer bet.

The Borough

OPEN.

Mon-Sat. 7:30am - 6:00pm
Sun. Closed

OVERVIEW.

Catergory
Artisanal Independent
Owner
Anita Le Roy
First opened
2001

COFFEE & EQUIPMENT.

Coffee roaster
Monmouth Coffee Company
Coffee machine
La Marzocco Linea,
2 groups x 2
Coffee grinder
Mazzer

Sister coffee shops.
Covent Garden / Bermondsey

COFFEE PRICING.

Espresso	£1.30 / £1.80
Cappucino	£2.30
Latte	£2.30
Flat white	£2.30

FOOD.

Help yourself to bread and jam
on the communal tables, or try
a croissant or brioche from
the counter

Also serve single origin filter coffee.
Monmouth Coffee Company roastery
located nearby in Bermondsey

CONTACT.

+44(0)20 7645 3562
www.monmouthcoffee.co.uk
beans@monmouthcoffee.co.uk

RATING.

COFFEE 4.75 / 5	
OVERALL 4.50 / 5	

ScooterCaffè

132 Lower Marsh, SE1 7AE ....

The brainchild of New Zealander and ex-aircraft engineer Craig O'Dwyer, ScooterCaffé started life as a Vespa workshop. Sit back and admire Craig's collection of vintage machinery parts as you enjoy a coffee made from a fully functional 1957 Faema espresso machine. With a moody basement area that hosts movie, music and comedy nights and a sunny courtyard out the back, you can feel at home here any time of day or night. Better still, a bring-your-own food policy means the menu is up to you. If retro is your thing, check this place out.

OPEN.

Mon-Thu.	8:30am - 11:00pm
Fri.	8:30am - 12:00am
Sat.	10:00am - 12:00am
Sun.	Closed

OVERVIEW.

Catergory
Artisanal Independent
Owner / Head barista
Craig O'Dwyer
First opened
2009

COFFEE & EQUIPMENT.

Coffee roaster
Londinium
Coffee machine
1957 Faema, 3 groups
Coffee grinder
Quick Mill, Omer (Vintage)

COFFEE PRICING.

Espresso	£1.50 / £2.00
Cappucino	£1.90
Latte	£1.90
Flat white	£1.90

FOOD.

Bring-your-own food policy.
Some sweets and snacks available

CONTACT.

+44(0)20 7620 1421
scootercaffe@googlemail.com

RATING.

COFFEE 4.25 / 5	🫘🫘🫘🫘🫘
OVERALL 4.25 / 5	★★★★☆

You Don't Bring Me Flowers

15 Staplehurst Road, SE13 5ND ....

This quaint venue doubles as both a florist and coffee house. The beautiful scent of fresh flowers pervades throughout, and colourful bouquets brighten and warm the room. Antique furniture and ornaments decorate the interior and a small courtyard upstairs offers a quiet place to sit and enjoy coffee and cake.

OPEN.

Mon.	Closed
Tue-Fri.	8:00am - 6:00pm
Sat.	9:00am - 6:00pm
Sun.	10:00am - 5:00pm

OVERVIEW.

Catergory
Artisanal Independent
Owner
Lynne Noreledge
First opened
2004

COFFEE & EQUIPMENT.

Coffee roaster
Darlington's
Coffee machine
La San Marco, 2 groups
Coffee grinder
Mazzer Luigi

COFFEE PRICING.

Espresso	£1.50
Cappucino	£1.90 / £2.20
Latte	£1.90 / £2.20
Flat white	£2.00

FOOD.

A range of pastries, cakes, tarts and
freshly made sandwiches

CONTACT.

+44(0)20 8297 2333
www.youdontbringmeflowers.co.uk
youdontbringmeflowers@hotmail.co.uk

RATING.

COFFEE
4.00 / 5

OVERALL
3.75 / 5

South West London

South West London is a cultural hot pot. Brixton is London's Afro-Caribbean home and its thriving refurbished market provides inspiration for many new initiatives. Neighbouring Clapham boasts a lively eating and drinking scene and is a place where families, young professionals and travellers congregate for entertainment.

Breads Etcetera

127 Clapham High Street, SW4 7SS ....

OPEN.

Tue-Sat.	10:00am - 10:00pm
Sun.	10:00am - 4:00pm

> Now **source & roast their own coffee** under the name **88 Coffee Company**

Breads Etcetera pride themselves on their award-winning organic sourdough breads, and the enticing bakery aroma alone is enough to draw you through the doors of this café. Weekend breakfast is a major event as trendy hungover locals debrief over coffee and DIY toast. Keep an eye out for the new Breads Etcetera bakery, coffee shop and roastery opening soon in Brixton Village Market.

FOOD.

Renowned for their sourdough breads and weekend brunch

CONTACT.

+44(0)77 1764 2812
daniel@breadsetceterabakery.com

Sister coffee shops.
Brixton Village Market

OVERVIEW.

Catergory
Bakery Coffee Shop
Owner
Daniel Fiteni and Kurt Anderson
Head barista
Daniel Fiteni
First opened
2005

COFFEE & EQUIPMENT.

Coffee roaster
88 Coffee Company
Coffee machine
Brugnetti CDE, 2 groups
Coffee grinder
Brugnetti

COFFEE PRICING.

Espresso	£1.25 / £1.50
Cappucino	£2.25
Latte	£2.25
Flat white	£2.25

RATING.

COFFEE 4.00 / 5	🫘🫘🫘🫘🫘
OVERALL 4.00 / 5	★★★★☆

Brew

45 Northcote Road, SW11 1NJ ....

OPEN.

Mon-Sat. 7:00am - 5:30pm
Sun. 7:30am - 5:30pm

A favourite amongst the Northcote Road set, Brew is a cheerful antidote to the many chain coffee stores nearby. Simple and homely, Brew offers Union coffee and a comprehensive breakfast and lunch menu in a breezy, laid-back environment. A great place to enjoy a coffee as you sit and watch the world go by.

FOOD.

Antipodean-style menu including poached eggs, salads, toasted pides and muffins

CONTACT.

+44(0)20 7585 2198
brewnorthcote@gmail.com

Sister coffee shops.
Brew (Borough Market)

OVERVIEW.

Catergory
Artisanal Independent
Owner
Jason Wells and Tim Molema
Head barista
Angela Florin
First Opened
2008

COFFEE & EQUIPMENT.

Coffee roaster
Union Hand-Roasted
Coffee machine
La Marzocco Linea, 2 groups
Coffee grinder
Mazzer Luigi srl

COFFEE PRICING.

Espresso	£1.50 / £1.80
Cappucino	£2.00
Latte	£2.00
Flat white	£2.00

RATING.

COFFEE 4.25 / 5	🫘 🫘 🫘 🫘 🫘
OVERALL 4.00 / 5	★ ★ ★ ★ ★

Daylesford Organic Pimlico Road

44B Pimlico Road, SW1W 8LP

OPEN.

Mon-Sat. 8:00am - 8:00pm
Sun. 10:00am - 4:00pm

Daylesford Organic on Pimlico Road combines a number of elements to create an experience of organics and 'slow food'. The venue encompasses a café, grocer, bakery, cookery school and homewares store over three spacious, light and relaxing floors. Enjoy a coffee and wholesome directly-sourced lunch, and watch it all happen in the basement where the kitchen is on view though full-length windows.

FOOD.

Organic, seasonal and fresh produce dircect from Daylesford farms. Menu includes soup, salads, heartier mains and a selection of puddings

CONTACT.

+44(0)20 7881 8060
www.daylesfordorganic.com
enquiries@daylesfordorganic.com

Sister coffee shops.
Notting Hill / Selfridges / Gloucestershire

OVERVIEW.

Catergory
Chain
Owner
Carole Bamford
First opened
2007

COFFEE & EQUIPMENT.

Coffee roaster
Union Hand-Roasted
Coffee machine
La Marzocco Firenze Linea, 2 groups
Coffee grinder
Mazze Luigi srl Super Jolly

COFFEE PRICING.

Espresso	£2.00 / £2.50
Cappucino	£2.50 / £3.25
Latte	£2.50 / £3.25
Flat white	£2.50 / £3.25

RATING.

COFFEE 4.00 / 5	🫘 🫘 🫘 🫘 🫘
OVERALL 4.00 / 5	★ ★ ★ ★ ☆

Di'Zain

277 New Kings Road, SW6 4RD ....

Di'Zain is a stylish café in an area otherwise seriously lacking quality coffee shops. The contrasting black and white interior is complemented by full length mirrors to create a sophisticated environment to enjoy a flat white. Chillout music adds to the trendy ambience, staff are friendly (and more often than not, Australian) and the brunch menu offers something to suit all tastes. Soon to also open evenings as a wine bar, Di'Zain is a welcome addition to the burgeoning south-west London scene.

FOOD.

Antipodean-style breakfast and brunch, sandwiches, salads, and a selection of more substantial mains

CONTACT.

+44(0)20 7751 9711
www.di-zain.co.uk
info@di-zain.co.uk

OPEN.

Mon-Fri. 7:30am - 6:00pm
Sat-Sun. 9:00am - 6:00pm

OVERVIEW.

Catergory
Artisanal Independent
Owner
Katie Newton-Darby, Albi Ison and Emily Beeren
Head barista
Albi Ison
First Opened
2009

COFFEE & EQUIPMENT.

Coffee roaster
Darlington's
Coffee machine
La Marzocco Linea, 2 groups
Coffee grinder
Mazzer Luigi srl

COFFEE PRICING.

Espresso	£1.80
Cappucino	£2.50
Latte	£2.60
Flat white	£2.50

RATING.

COFFEE 4.00 / 5	
OVERALL 4.00 / 5	

133

Federation Coffee

Unit 77-78 Brixton Village Market, Coldharbour Lane, SW9 8PS ......

OPEN.

Mon-Fri.	8:00am - 5:00pm
Sat.	9:30am - 5:00pm
Sun.	9:30am - 4:00pm

Frustrated by a lack of good coffee shops in their local area, New Zealanders George Wallace and Nick Coates decided to take matters into their own hands. Federation Coffee was born in the redeveloped Brixton Village Market in early 2010. Serving Nude Espresso coffee and home-made baked treats, their focus is on quality and simplicity. Definitely one to watch as word spreads – get in early before everyone else discovers Federation Coffee.

FOOD.

A small selection of home-made cakes, muffins and biscuits

CONTACT.

www.federationcoffee.com
info@federationcoffee.com

OVERVIEW.

Catergory
Artisanal Independent
Owner / Head barista
George Wallace and Nick Coates
First opened
2010

COFFEE & EQUIPMENT.

Coffee roaster
Nude Espresso
Coffee machine
La Marzocco Linea, 3 groups
Coffee grinder
Anfim Super Caimano

COFFEE PRICING.

Espresso	£1.40
Cappucino	£2.00
Latte	£2.00
Flat white	£2.00

RATING.

COFFEE 4.50 / 5	OVERALL 4.00 / 5

Gail's Battersea

64 Northcote Road, SW11 6QL ....

OPEN.

Mon-Fri.	7:30am - 7:30pm
Sat-Sun.	8:00am - 7:00pm

Gail's Battersea has proven to be very popular since opening in 2009. A tempting range of freshly made salads, sandwiches and baked goods greet you at the entrance, and the spotless kitchen is on display as you walk through to the large seating area out the back. Loved by mothers with young children as a place to seek some respite and catch up with friends over coffee and cake.

FOOD.

A fresh and colourful range of sandwiches, salads, bakery treats and cakes made on site

CONTACT.

+44(0)20 7924 6330
www.gailsbread.co.uk
battersea@gailsbread.co.uk

Sister coffee shops.
Hampstead/ Notting Hill / St Johns Wood / Queen's Park / Chiswick

OVERVIEW.

Catergory
Chain
Owner
Ran Avidan and Tom Molnar
Head barista
Morika Gasparova
First Opened
2009

COFFEE & EQUIPMENT.

Coffee roaster
Union Hand-Roasted
Coffee machine
La Marzocco GB5, 3 groups
Coffee grinder
Mazzer Super Jolly

COFFEE PRICING.

Espresso	£1.65 / £1.95
Cappucino	£2.35 / £2.95
Latte	£2.35 / £2.95
Flat white	£2.35 / £2.95

RATING.

COFFEE	4.00 / 5
OVERALL	4.00 / 5

The Goodbench

14D Market Row, Brixton Market, SW9 8LB

The Goodbench is a brand new addition to the redeveloped Brixton Market. With a focus on retail coffee and a rotating selection of beans available for purchase, it's a great place to choose your coffee for home, as you enjoy a rich flat white in the welcoming store. Climb the ladder if you're game and settle in to the comfy loft area. The same team run a coffee cart outside the Clapham Common tube station.

OPEN.

Mon-Wed.	8:00am - 5:00pm
Thu.	8:00am - 8:00pm
Fri, Sat.	8:00am - 5:00pm
Sun.	Closed

OVERVIEW.

Catergory
Artisanal Independent
Owner / Head barista
Haroon Hassan
First opened
2010

COFFEE & EQUIPMENT.

Coffee roaster
Traders Coffee Ltd
Coffee machine
Estoria Perla, 2 groups
Coffee grinder
Mazzer x 2

Sister coffee shops.
Cart outside Clapham Common
tube station

COFFEE PRICING.

Espresso	£1.50
Cappucino	£2.00
Latte	£2.00
Flat white	£2.00

FOOD.

A small selection of home-made
cakes and cookies

CONTACT.

+44(0)75 9522 4322
haroon@thegoodbench.com

Range of beans
available for
purchase

RATING.

COFFEE	4.25 / 5
OVERALL	4.25 / 5

Le Pain Quotidien Parsons Green

70 Parsons Green Lane, SW6 4HU ....

OPEN.

Mon-Fri.	7:00am - 10:00pm
Sat.	8:00am - 10:00pm
Sun.	8:00am - 9:00pm

Le Pain Quotidien is an airy and welcoming boulangerie and café on Parsons Green Lane. Booth seats in recycled horse stables are a charming feature, along with the signature LPQ communal table highlighted with pretty drop lights. The atmosphere inside is refined and peaceful, with classical music, lofty high ceilings and exposed brick walls. Enjoy a coffee while you linger over a lazy breakfast.

FOOD.

Organic sourdough breads and pastries made fresh on site daily. An all-day menu of tartines, salads, hot dishes and sweet snacks

CONTACT.

+44(0)20 7486 6154
www.lepainquotidien.co.uk
parsonsgreen@lpquk.biz

Sister coffee shops.
15 other stores in London

OVERVIEW.

Catergory
Bakery Coffee Shop
Owner
Le Pain Quotidien
First opened
2009

Also serve **filter coffee**

COFFEE & EQUIPMENT.

Coffee roaster
Miko Puro
Coffee machine
Faema Emblema, 2 groups and Faema E61 Legend, 2 groups
Coffee grinder
Mazzer Luigi srl x 2

COFFEE PRICING.

Espresso	£1.60 / £2.00
Cappucino	£2.20 / £3.00
Latte	£2.20 / £3.00

RATING.

COFFEE 3.50 / 5	
OVERALL 3.75 / 5	

The Roastery (Bullet Coffee Cartel)

789 Wandsworth Road, SW8 3JQ ....

OPEN.

Mon-Fri.   7:30am - 3:30pm
Sat-Sun.   9:00am - 3:30pm

Don't let the small size of this café fool you – there's plenty going on inside. Bullet Coffee Cartel do their roasting on site, and you can watch the process from beginning to end. The vibe is relaxed and casual, with retro-styled decor and ambient music. A range of beans and ground coffee is available for purchase, and Bullet also wholesale to other venues around London.

FOOD.

A new brunch menu, home-made cakes, biscuits and snacks

CONTACT.

+44(0)20 7350 1961
www.bullet-coffee.com
info@bullet-coffee.com

OVERVIEW.

Catergory
Artisanal Independent
Owner
Phil Ross
Head barista
Nick MacKinnon
First opened
2009

COFFEE & EQUIPMENT.

Coffee roaster
Bullet Coffee Cartel
Coffee machine
Modified/PID La Marzocco Linea, 3 groups
Coffee grinder
Mazzer x 3

COFFEE PRICING.

Espresso	£1.50
Cappucino	£2.30
Latte	£2.30
Flat white	£2.30

RATING.

COFFEE 4.25 / 5	🫘🫘🫘🫘🫘
OVERALL 3.75 / 5	★★★★★

Call us picky, but we like our coffee...

....made with 100% arabica beans. We want them to be a perfect blend of earthy dark spice beans from the tropics of Sumatra, soft berry jam flavoured beans from the warm Ethiopian climate, dry toast and golden straw scented beans from the altitude of Peru and those all important green fruit notes from those gorgeous Honduran beans. And we insist that the beans used in our M&S Café espresso blend are not only Fairtrade certified and organic, but Rainforest Alliance Certified* too. We also insist the beans are checked at every stage of the production process. And when that's done we want the beans packed immediately, no hanging about, in order to seal in the freshness. Finally, we want our coffee prepared by an expertly trained barista, to ensure that the coffee isn't burnt and bitter and someone who knows how to make the milk perfectly frothy.

And don't even get us started on the caramel flapjack.

Fairtrade certified

Organic

Rainforest Alliance Certified™

M&S Café

Kensington & Chelsea

This district is home to some of London's wealthiest residents, world-renowned museums and of course chic department stores Harrods and Harvey Nichols. Well-heeled locals mix with curious tourists in the area's many cafés, restaurants and cocktail bars.

Andronicas World of Coffee Harrods

Fourth Floor Harrods, 87–135 Brompton Road, SW1X 7XL ···············

Andronicas is a sleek coffee house located on the fourth floor of Harrods department store. It's all about the coffee here – as well as the drink-in menu a large variety of beans are available for purchase, alongside artfully displayed equipment for home use. Andronicas is a destination in its own right, or a welcome retreat for weary Harrods shoppers to stop and recharge.

Sister coffee shops.
Covent Garden / ExCel Royal Victoria Dock / Peterborough

OPEN.

Mon-Sat. 10:00am - 7:00pm
Sun. 12:00pm - 6:00pm

OVERVIEW.

Catergory
Retail & Leisure
Owner
Andrew Knight
Head barista
Kamel Deramchi
First opened
2007

COFFEE & EQUIPMENT.

Coffee roaster
Andronicas
Coffee machine
Mirage Veloce, 2 groups
Coffee grinder
Mahlkönig

COFFEE PRICING.

Espresso £1.75
Cappucino £2.00 / £2.50 / £3.00
Latte £2.00 / £2.50 / £3.00

FOOD.
Fresh salads, sandwiches, antipasto
and desserts

CONTACT.
+44(0)20 7730 1234
www.andronicasworldofcoffee.com
coffee@andronicas.com

RATING.

| COFFEE 4.25 / 5 | 🫘 🫘 🫘 🫘 🫘 |
| OVERALL 3.50 / 5 | ★ ★ ★ ⯪ ☆ |

Aubaine Brompton Cross
260-262 Brompton Road, SW3 2AS

Aubaine is a lively French restaurant, always busy and ever-popular with the well-dressed Chelsea crowd. Inside is spacious, light-filled and buzzing with chatter. Come down on a Sunday morning for delicious coffee and brunch at one of the outside tables, and watch the passing crowd stroll by in the sunshine.

Sister coffee shops.
Heddon Street / Selfridges
Kensington High Street
(opening January 2011)

Image supplied by Aubaine

OPEN.

Mon-Sat. 8:00am - 10:30pm
Sun &
Bank Hols. 9:00am - 10:00pm

OVERVIEW.

Catergory
Eatery
Owner
Hani Nakkash
First Opened
2004

COFFEE & EQUIPMENT.

Coffee roaster
Musetti
Coffee machine
Gaggia, 3 goups
Coffee grinder
Gaggia

COFFEE PRICING.

Espresso	£1.80 / £2.65
Cappucino	£2.80 / £3.25
Latte	£2.80 / £3.25
Flat white	£2.80 / £3.25

FOOD.

French-inspired breakfast, brunch
and main meals, as well as desserts
and freshly baked bread

CONTACT.

+44(0)20 7052 0100
www.aubaine.co.uk
info@aubaine.co.uk

RATING.

COFFEE 3.75 / 5	
OVERALL 3.75 / 5	

Brompton Quarter Brasserie

225 Brompton Road, SW3 2EJ

Stylish modern eatery Brompton Quarter Brasserie sums up the Knightsbridge scene very nicely. With an immaculate open dining space, crisp white walls and colour-changing bar lights, this is a place to see and be seen. A great place to take a date when out to impress.

Sister coffee shops.
Bread Boutique

OPEN.
Mon-Sun. 7:30am - 11:00pm

OVERVIEW.
Catergory
Eatery
Owner
Doron Zilkha and Valeria Zilkha
Head barista
Alicia
First opened
2006

COFFEE & EQUIPMENT.
Coffee roaster
Illy
Coffee machine
Wega, 3 groups
Coffee grinder
Mazzer Luigi srl

COFFEE PRICING.

Espresso	£1.95 / £2.95
Cappucino	£2.95
Latte	£2.95

FOOD.
Fresh salads, sandwiches, antipasto
and desserts

CONTACT.
+44(0)20 7225 2107
www.bqbrasserie.com
info@bqbrasserie.com

RATING.

COFFEE
4.00 / 5

OVERALL
3.75 / 5

Caffè Nero Gloucester Road

119-121 Gloucester Road, SW7 4TE ....

OPEN.

Mon-Fri.	6:30am - 9:00pm
Sat.	7:00am - 9:00pm
Sun.	7:30am - 9:00pm

This new Caffè Nero is a classy and inviting outlet on a busy South Kensington corner block.
The interior is modern and understated, with plenty of space and light. Favourite spots are the dangerously comfortable oversized red leather chairs, and the outside tables for people-watching on a sunny day.

FOOD.

Iced drinks, sandwiches, soups, pastas, salads, cakes, muffins, biscuits and pastries

CONTACT.

+44(0)20 7244 8578
www.caffenero.com
enquiries@caffenero.com

Sister coffee shops.
Over 400 UK outlets

OVERVIEW.

Catergory
Chain
Owner
Caffè Nero Group Ltd
First Opened
2010

COFFEE & EQUIPMENT.

Coffee roaster
Caffè Nero
Coffee machine
Faema E91 Ambassador, 4 groups
Coffee grinder
Mazzer Super Jolly

COFFEE PRICING.

Espresso	£1.40 / £1.70
Cappucino	£1.75 / £2.15 / £2.45
Latte	£1.75 / £2.15 / £2.45

RATING.

COFFEE 4.00 / 5	
OVERALL 4.00 / 5	

Coffee Plant

180 Portobello Road, W11 2EB

OPEN.

Mon-Sat.	7:45am - 5:30pm
Sun.	9:00am - 4:30pm

Coffee Plant is a funky coffee shop on Notting Hill's bustling Portobello Road. It began life as a roastery, which can now be found in Acton and supplies not only their own coffee shop but several others around London. Retail coffee is ground to order for purchase here at the shop. The clientele ranges from young backpackers to middle-aged businessmen and everything in between.

FOOD.

A selection of basic sandwiches and pastries, organic confectionary and chocolate

CONTACT.

+44(0)20 7221 8137
www.coffee.uk.com

OVERVIEW.

Catergory
Artisanal Independent
Owner
Ian Henshall
First opened
2000

COFFEE & EQUIPMENT.

Coffee roaster
Coffee Plant
Coffee machine
Iberital L'adri, 2 groups x 2
Coffee grinder
Macap

COFFEE PRICING.

Espresso	£1.00 / £1.40
Cappucino	£1.60 / £1.80 / £2.00
Latte	£1.60 / £1.80 / £2.00
Flat white	£1.60 / £1.80 / £2.00

RATING.

COFFEE 3.75 / 5	🫘 🫘 🫘 🫘 🫘
OVERALL 3.75 / 5	★ ★ ★ ✦ ★

Garden Café at Buckingham Palace

West Terrace, Buckingham Palace, SW1A 1AA ....

Image supplied by Garden Café

OPEN.
Only open during the Summer Opening of Buckingham Palace, Palace admission fees apply.

Mon-Sun. 9:45am - 6:00pm
(last admission 3:45pm)

This is the closest most of us will ever get to having a coffee with The Queen. The Garden Café is positioned on the terrace overlooking the lush green gardens of Buckingham Palace, and is the final stop on The Palace Summer Opening tours. Coffees come topped with a crown dusted in chocolate for that Royal touch.

FOOD.

A selction of cakes, sandwiches, scones and Buckingham Palace icecream are available

CONTACT.

+44(0)20 7839 1377
www.royalcollection.org.uk
bookinginfo@royalcollection.org.uk

Sister coffee shops.
Café at the Palace, Holyrood House Edinburgh

OVERVIEW.

Catergory
Grand Traditional
Owner
The Royal Collection
First Opened
2010

COFFEE & EQUIPMENT.

Coffee roaster
Grand Café by First Choice Coffee

COFFEE PRICING.

Espresso	£1.50
Cappucino	£2.65
Latte	£2.65

RATING.

COFFEE 2.75 / 5	
OVERALL 4.00 / 5	★★★★☆

150

Kensington Square Kitchen

9 Kensington Square, W8 5EP ·······························

OPEN.

Mon-Sat. 8:30am - 5:00pm
Sun. 9:30am - 4:30pm

Also open for dinner during Summer
(May-Oct)

This charming café in leafy Kensington Square is small but filled with character. The ground floor seating area spills onto the pavement providing a great vantage point from which to observe the Kensington set whilst sipping your latte. Downstairs, a cocoon-like space provides a more intimate venue for that special lunch or coffee date. Brunch here is ever-popular and the menu constantly changes depending what's in season.

FOOD.

Appetising cooked breakfasts, an all-day brunch menu and daily salads and lunch specials. Open for dinner during summer

CONTACT.

+44(0)20 7938 2598
www.kensingtonsquarekitchen.co.uk
info@kensingtonsquarekitchen.co.uk

OVERVIEW.

Catergory
Eatery
Owner
Sara Adams
Head barista
Per Bossen-Moller
First opened
2007

COFFEE & EQUIPMENT.

Coffee roaster
Monmouth Coffee Company
Coffee machine
La Marzocco Linea, 2 groups
Coffee grinder
Mazzer Luigi srl Super Jolly

COFFEE PRICING.

Espresso	£1.75
Cappucino	£2.50
Latte	£2.50
Flat white	£2.50

RATING.

COFFEE 4.00 / 5	
OVERALL 3.75 / 5	

Ladurée Harrods
87/135 Brompton Road, SW1X 7XL

If opulent indulgence is your thing, a visit to Ladurée Harrods is a must. Occupying a ground floor site in one of the world's most well-known department stores, Ladurée is a visual delight. All manner of immaculately presented sweets and treats are on display to tempt your tastebuds. Have a seat in the indoor dining area, or if the skies are clear, take an outdoor table and soak up the atmosphere in style.

Images supplied by Ladurée

COFFEE PRICING.

Espresso	£1.95 / £2.85
Cappucino	£2.85
Latte	£2.85

FOOD.

Ladurée are famous for their macaroons and other French patisserie specialties; a savoury menu is also on offer

CONTACT.

+44(0)20 3155 0111
www.laduree.fr

OPEN.

Mon-Sat.	9:00am - 9:00pm
Sun.	11:30pm - 6:00pm

OVERVIEW.

Catergory
Grand Traditional
Owner
David Holder
Head barista
Benedict MacDonald
First Opened
2005

COFFEE & EQUIPMENT.

Coffee roaster
Lavazza
Coffee machine
WMS
Coffee grinder
WMS

Sister coffee shops.
16 stores globally

RATING.

COFFEE	3.50 / 5
OVERALL	4.25 / 5

Lisboa Patisserie
57 Golborne Road, W10 5NR

OPEN.
Mon-Sun. 7:00am - 7:30pm

Lisboa Patisserie is a no-frills Portugese bakery with a mouth-watering selection of cakes, pastries and traditional baked products. The displays are simple but, judging by the number of people coming through the doors, there is something special going on here. Coffee is served Portugese-style, and is a steal at £1.10 for a latte or cappucino.

FOOD.
Traditional Portugese cakes, pastries and bakery goods

CONTACT.
+44(0)20 8968 5242

OVERVIEW.
Catergory
Bakery Coffee Shop
Owner
Carlos Gomes
First opened
1986

COFFEE & EQUIPMENT.
Coffee roaster
Sical
Coffee machine
Wega, 2 groups and La Cimbali, 2 groups
Coffee grinder
Wega Max

COFFEE PRICING.
Espresso	£1.00 / £2.00
Cappucino	£1.10 / £1.25
Latte	£1.10
Flat white	£1.00

RATING.

COFFEE 3.50 / 5	
OVERALL 3.50 / 5	

Tom's Deli

226 Westbourne Grove, W11 2RH

Image supplied by Tom's Deli

OPEN.

Mon-Fri.	8:00am - 7:30pm
Sat.	8:00am - 6:30pm
Sun.	9:00am - 6:30pm

This cheerful Notting Hill café has developed quite the reputation as the best breakfast spot around. With bright decor, vinyl booth seats and a cosy outdoor patio, Tom's Deli is welcoming and fun. A great spot to meet friends for coffee or a hearty brunch, and pick up some treats from the deli downstairs on the way out.

FOOD.

As well as the popular breakfast menu, an impressive spread of sandwiches, salads and cakes

CONTACT.

+44(0)20 7221 8818
www.tomsdelilondon.co.uk
office@tomsdeli.co.uk

Sister coffee shops.
3 other restaurants in London

OVERVIEW.

Catergory
Eatery
Owner
Tom Conran
First Opened
1990

Deli & grocer located downstairs

COFFEE & EQUIPMENT.

Coffee roaster
Andronicas
Coffee machine
La Marzocco Linea, 2 groups and Faema E-91 Diplomat, 3 groups
Coffee grinder
Mazzer Super Jolly

COFFEE PRICING.

Espresso	£1.65 / £1.80
Cappucino	£2.30
Latte	£2.30
Flat white	£2.30

RATING.

COFFEE 4.25 / 5	🫘🫘🫘🫘◗
OVERALL 4.00 / 5	★★★★☆

Tomtom Coffee House

114 Ebury Street, SW1W 9QD

Tomtom Coffee House is tucked away from the hustle and bustle of Belgravia's busy streets. Inside, a large communal table helps generate a neighbourly feel and the atmosphere is very European, with accents of all descriptions heard from staff and customers alike. Tomtom roast their own coffee, and several house blends are available for purchase. The coffee house will soon be open in the evenings as a cocktail bar.

OPEN.

Mon-Fri.	8:00am - 9:00pm
Sat.	9:00am - 9:00pm
Sun.	9:00am - 5:00pm

OVERVIEW.

Catergory
Artisanal Independent
Owner
Tom Assheton and Giles Dick-Read
Head barista
Jana Zubcakova
First opened
2007

COFFEE & EQUIPMENT.

Coffee roaster
Tomtom (Charles Reid)
Coffee machine
La Marzocco Linea, 2 groups
Coffee grinder
Mahlkönig

COFFEE PRICING.

Espresso	£1.70 / £2.20
Cappucino	£2.50 / £2.80
Latte	£2.50 / £2.80
Flat white	£2.50 / £2.80

FOOD.

All-day breakfast, toasted sarnies, salads, soups, dips platters and baked goodies

CONTACT.

+44(0)20 7730 1771
www.tomtom.co.uk
coffee@tomtom.co.uk

RATING.

COFFEE 4.25 / 5

OVERALL 4.00 / 5

West London

The neighbourhoods of West London have a cosy village feel, dotted with upmarket restaurants, local cafés and fashion boutiques. These venues provide welcome respite from the hectic pace of central London.

Baker & Spice Maida Vale

20 Clifton Road, W9 1SU

OPEN.

Mon-Sat. 7:00am - 7:00pm
Sun. 8:00am - 6:00pm

Baker & Spice café in Maida Vale has a lovely neighbourhood feel, as the meeting place of choice for local residents out for a post-gym coffee or lazy lunch. There are several outdoor tables for alfresco dining in the sun, or try the bench seating along the window to keep an eye on passers-by. A delicious spread of deli-style food is on tempting display.

FOOD.

Freshly-made salads, croissants, bakery treats and afternoon tea are available

CONTACT.

+44(0)20 7289 2499
www.bakerandspice.uk.com
maidavale@bakerandspice.co.uk

Sister coffee shops.
Belgravia / Chelsea

OVERVIEW.

Catergory
Chain
Owner
Patisserie Holdings Ltd
Head barista
Raj Rathold
First opened
2007

COFFEE & EQUIPMENT.

Coffee roaster
Musetti
Coffee machine
Gaggia D90, 3 groups
Coffee grinder
Mazzer

COFFEE PRICING.

Espresso	£2.00
Cappucino	£2.90
Latte	£2.90
Flat white	£2.90

RATING.

COFFEE 3.50 / 5

OVERALL 4.00 / 5

Gail's Queen's Park

75 Salusbury Road, NW6 6NH ....

OPEN.

Mon-Fri.	7:00am - 8:00pm
Sat-Sun.	8:00am - 8:00pm

The newest Gail's has created considerable buzz around the Queen's Park neighbourhood. Gail's signature display of appetising sandwiches, cakes and baked treats draws you inside to a cosy seating area to the rear. The crisp, clean finish creates a modern upbeat feel inside. A great place to escape for a quiet coffee, long lunch or afternoon treat.

FOOD.

A fresh and colourful range of sandwiches, salads, bakery treats and cakes made on site

CONTACT.

+44(0)20 7625 0068
www.gailsbread.co.uk
qp@gailsbread.co.uk

Sister coffee shops.
Hampstead / Notting Hill / St Johns Wood / Battersea / Chiswick

OVERVIEW.

Catergory
Chain
Owner
Ran Avidan and Tom Molnar
Head barista
Elia Cordaro
First Opened
2010

COFFEE & EQUIPMENT.

Coffee roaster
Union Hand-Roasted
Coffee machine
La Marzocco Linea, 3 groups
Coffee grinder
Mazzer Super Jolly

COFFEE PRICING.

Espresso	£1.65 / £1.95
Cappucino	£2.35 / £2.95
Latte	£2.35 / £2.95
Flat white	£2.35 / £2.95

RATING.

COFFEE 4.00 / 5	
OVERALL 3.75 / 5	

Indie Coffee

50 Church Street Market, NW8 8EP ....

Image supplied by Indie Coffee

OPEN.
Tue-Sat. 8:00am - 3:00pm

An unexpected find in the midst of the Church Street Market, this quaint coffee cart first opened in 2009. Owner Peter Duggan has since carved out a niche serving what many say is the best espresso-based coffee in the area. Peter's personal approach to his craft and genuine customer service have won him many loyal customers.

FOOD.

Local handmade biscuits

CONTACT.

+44(0)78 2506 8909
indie.coffee@yahoo.com

OVERVIEW.

Catergory
Stall / Cart / Kiosk
Owner / head barista
Peter Duggan
First opened
2009

COFFEE & EQUIPMENT.

Coffee roaster
Square Mile Coffee Roasters
Coffee machine
La Marzocco Linea, 2 groups
Coffee grinder
Anfim

COFFEE PRICING.

Espresso	£1.00 / £1.40
Cappucino	£1.90
Latte	£1.90
Flat white	£1.90

RATING.

COFFEE 4.00 / 5	🫘 🫘 🫘 🫘 🫘

Acidity: one of the principal categories used by professional tasters to determine the quality of a coffee or blend along with flavour, aroma and body. Usually the pleasant tartness of a fine coffee and not the pH level.

Affogato: a coffee-based dessert - usually a scoop of vanilla ice cream topped with a shot of hot espresso.

Americano, Caffè Americano: an espresso with hot water added.

Arabica, Coffea Arabica: the earliest cultivated species of coffee tree and still the most widely grown. It produces approximately 70% of the world's coffee and is dramatically superior in cup quality to the other principal commercial coffee species 'Coffea Canephora' or 'Robusta'.

Aroma: the way the coffee smells. Aroma is one of the principal categories used by professional tasters to determine the quality of a particular coffee or blend. Examples of aromas include earthy, spicy, floral and nutty.

Blend: a combination of coffees from different countries and regions in order to achieve a taste that no single coffee can offer alone.

Body: the heaviness, thickness or relative weight of the coffee on the tongue when tasted. Body is one of the principal categories used by professional tasters to determine the quality of a coffee or blend.

Brew Group: in an espresso machine, the brew group contains the portafilter and group head. It needs to be heated in order to brew the espresso.

Brew Temperature: is dependent on the extraction method. For filter and French Press water should be just below boiling, and the consensus is that espresso should be brewed with water at 88-120oC.

Brew Time: is the time it takes for an espresso to pour from the portafilter spout and is one of the key indicators of a good espresso shot. The guideline for an espresso is 25-30 seconds.

Café au Lait: one-third drip coffee with two-thirds hot frothed milk.

Café con Leche: a traditional Spanish coffee where the espresso is served with scalded milk.

Caffè Mocha or Mocha: similar to a caffè latte but with added chocolate syrup or powder and often topped with whipped cream.

Caffeine: an odourless bitter alkaloid responsible for the stimulating effect of coffee and tea.

Cappuccino: one third espresso, one third steamed milk and one third frothed milk. A traditional Italian cappuccino is 4.5oz, but in the UK they are usually larger. Often topped with powdered chocolate or cinnamon.

Cortado: a traditional Spanish coffee made with a shot of espresso and a dash of warm milk to reduce acidity.

Crema: the pale brown foam covering the surface of an espresso, created by the dispersion of gases in liquid at high pressure. A sign of a well extracted shot.

Cupping: a method by which professional tasters perform sensory evaluation of samples of coffee beans. Water is poured over ground beans and the coffee is left to stand for a few minutes to allow extraction. The taster smells the coffee then slurps it directly from the cup. The grounds are still within the liquid so tasters often spit it out after allowing the flavour, body and acidity to register in the mouth.

Dispersion Screen: an essential part of the brew group, it ensures the correct dispensing of brewing water over a wide pattern into the portafilter and filter basket.

Dosage: the amount of ground coffee for each brewing method. For espresso, dosage should be 7g per 1.5oz shot.

Doppio: a double espresso, or three to six ounces of straight espresso.

Drip or Filter Method: brewing method allowing hot water to settle through a bed of ground coffee, either with or without a filter paper.

Espresso: the basis for the majority of coffee beverages in coffee shops, made from hot water forced at high pressure through 7g of finely ground coffee to produce 1.5oz of extracted beverage.

Extraction: the act of turning water into brewed coffee or espresso by allowing coffee to sit in hot water for a period of time or forcing hot water through ground coffee.

Filter Basket: sits in the portafilter and holds a bed of ground coffee. It has a multitude of tiny holes in the bottom to allow the extracted beverage to seep through and pour into a cup.

Filter Method: any brewing method in which water filters through a bed of ground coffee. Most commonly used to describe drip method brewers utilising a paper filter to separate grounds from brewed coffee.

cont.

Flat White: an espresso-based beverage hailing from Australia and New Zealand made with a single or double shot of espresso and finely steamed milk (or microfoam). Typically served as an 8oz drink, a flat white is similar to a traditional Italian cappuccino and is often served with latte art.

Flavour: one of the principal categories used by professional tasters to determine the quality of a coffee or blend. It refers to the taste and notes such as citrus, nutty, earthy and exotic which describe the coffee.

French Press, Plunger Pot, Cafétiere: brewing method that separates spent grounds from brewed coffee by pressing them to the bottom of the brewing receptacle with a mesh plunger.

Froth/Foam: as milk is steamed using a steaming wand, air is introduced into the liquid resulting in the production of froth. To get the best froth the steam tip is held near the surface of the milk. As the steam agitates and heats the milk, it increases in volume and the wand tip is then moved up. By doing this it also draws air at high velocity into the milk, thus creating the foam or froth. Steamed milk and froth should be poured, not spooned out in clumps.

Green Coffee (Green Beans): unroasted coffee.

Grind: the extent to which whole bean coffee is ground will determine the resulting coffee brewed from it. A coarse grind should be used for a brewing method where the grounds will sit in the water for a period of time. A very fine grind is suited to high speed brewing or extraction methods such as espresso.

Grouphead: the part of the brew group containing the locking connector for the portafilter and the dispersion screen. An integral part of the espresso machine, the grouphead helps to maintain temperature stability in the machine essential for producing a perfect shot.

Latte or Caffè Latte: a shot of espresso combined with about three times as much hot milk topped with dry foamed milk.

Latte art: Created by pouring steamed milk into a shot of espresso and creating a pattern or design on the surface of the resulting latte.

Long Black: made by pulling a double shot of espresso over hot water. Similar to an Americano, except that unlike the Americano it retains the crema from the espresso and has a stronger flavour.

Macchiato: Either a serving of espresso 'stained' or marked with a small quantity of hot frothed milk (espresso macchiato) or a moderately tall (8oz) glass of hot frothed milk 'stained' with espresso (latte macchiato).

Macrofoam or Dry Foam: the type of foam created when steaming milk for a cappuccino or latte, where the milk is steamed in order to create visibly large bubbles.

Microfoam: an ideal standard for steamed milk used for espresso-based coffee drinks, particularly those with latte art. Microfoam is made using a steam wand on an espresso machine. Typically microfoam has much smaller bubbles than macrofoam.

Moka Pot or Stovetop: a manual method of making strong coffee, usually used on the stovetop. It brews by forcing hot water through a bed of coffee using the power and pressure of steam and produces a strong condensed shot of coffee.

Over Extracted: to make the perfect coffee water should be introduced for a set amount of time, depending on how coarse or fine the coffee beans have been ground. This term describes coffee that has had water exposed to ground coffee for too long, usually resulting in a bitter or burnt taste.

Percolation: any method of coffee brewing in which hot water percolates or filters down through a bed of ground coffee. The pumping percolator utilises the power of boiling water to force water up a tube and over a bed of ground coffee.

Piccolo: a version of a caffè latte served in a macchiato glass made from an espresso, topped with milk and 5mm of foam.

Pod: a self-contained, pre-ground, pre-pressed puck of ground coffee, usually sold individually wrapped inside a perforated paper filter. The pod is used in a specific type of coffee machine which extracts the coffee from it.

Portafilter (groupo): the device that holds a filter and finely ground coffee and facilitates quick attachment to an espresso machine. Water is forced through the portafilters allowing espresso to pour through the spout underneath.

Puck: after a shot of espresso has been brewed, the bed of coffee grounds forms a hard, compressed collection of coffee grounds resembling a hockey puck. Also referred to as a spent puck.

Coffee Glossary

cont.

Red Eye: a shot of espresso fortified with drip coffee.

Ristretto: a restricted shot using the same dose of grinds as a double espresso but with only about 1.50z (or less) of espresso, poured in the normal brewing time of 25-30 seconds. The result is a richer and more intense beverage.

Roast: the method by which green coffee is heated in order to produce consumable coffee. Roasting begins when the temperature inside the green bean reaches approximately 2000C (this varies between different varieties of beans). Caramelisation occurs as intense heat converts starches in the bean to simple sugars that begin to brown, creating the brown coffee bean.

Robusta, Coffea Canephora: the only significant competitor among cultivated coffee species to Coffea Arabica, robusta produces about 30% of the world's coffee. Robusta is grown at lower altitudes than Arabica and is a hardy, robust plant that often produces high yields. The flavour is often less refined and it has a much higher caffeine content than arabica.

Shot: a single brewed espresso.

Steam Wand: the visible external pipe found on most espresso machines used to froth and steam milk.

Tamp (tamping): the act of pressing and compacting a bed of loose finely ground coffee into the portafilter basket in preparation for brewing espresso. The harder the coffee is tamped, the tighter the puck and the harder it is to extract the coffee. If the coffee grounds are too loosely tamped the water will flow through too quickly.

Under Extracted: describes coffee that has not been exposed to water for long enough. The resulting brew is often weak and thin bodied.

Whole Bean Coffee: coffee that has been roasted but not yet ground.

cont.

Coffee Map Key

West End

	1	**Apostrophe** Baker Street
	2	**Caffè Nero** Bedford Street
	3	**Costa Coffee** Great Portland Street
TOP30	4	**Joe & The Juice** Regent Street
TOP30	5	**Kaffeine**
	6	**La Fromagerie** Marylebone
TOP30	7	**Lantana**
TOP30	8	**Monmouth Coffee Company** Covent Garden
	9	**Napket** Piccadilly
	10	**Notes, Music and Coffee**
	11	**Patisserie Valerie** Marylebone
TOP30	12	**The Providores**
	13	**Reynolds** Charlotte Street
	14	**Starbucks** Conduit Street
	15	**Tapped & Packed**

Soho

TOP30	16	**Bar Italia**
	17	**Brewed Boy Espresso**
TOP30	18	**Fernandez & Wells Café**
	19	**Fernandez & Wells Espresso Bar**
TOP30	20	**Flat White**
	21	**Foxcroft & Ginger**
	22	**Joe & The Juice** Broadwick Street
	23	**LJ Coffee House**
TOP30	24	**Milkbar**
TOP30	25	**Princi**
TOP30	26	**Sacred** Ganton Street

Farringdon & Clerkenwell

	27	**Brill**
TOP30	28	**Caravan**
TOP30	29	**Dose Espresso**
	30	**Farm Collective**
	31	**The Modern Pantry**

Camden & Islington

	32	**Bean About Town** Kentish Town
	33	**Bea's of Bloomsbury**
	34	**Coffee Circus**
TOP30	35	**The Espresso Room**
	36	**Fix**
	37	**Fleet River Bakery**
TOP30	38	**Ginger & White**
	39	**Goswell Road Coffee**
	40	**Lanka**
TOP30	41	**Look Mum No Hands!**
	42	**Melrose and Morgan** Primrose Hill
	43	**Merito Coffee Stall** Swiss Cottage Market
	44	**Ottolenghi** Islington
	45	**Pitch 42 @ Whitecross Street Market**
	46	**Sacred** Highbury Studios
TOP30	47	**Tina, We Salute You**
	48	**Tinderbox**
	49	**Wild and Wood Coffee**

Inner East

	50	**Albion**
TOP30	51	**Allpress Espresso Roastery**
TOP30	52	**Brick Lane Coffee**
	53	**Leila's**
TOP30	54	**Nude Espresso**
	55	**Prufrock Coffee at Present**
	56	**Taylor St Baristas** New Street
TOP30	57	**Taylor St Baristas** Old Broad Street

Hackney

	58	**Cà Phê VN** (Saigon Street Café)
TOP30	59	**Climpson & Sons**
	60	**Columbia Road Coffee Cart**
	61	**The Container Café**
TOP30	62	**The Counter Café**
	63	**The Hackney Pearl**
	64	**Hurwundeki Café**
	65	**Lemon Monkey**
	66	**Merito Coffee Stall** Broadway Market
	67	**Pavilion**
TOP30	68	**Taste of Bitter Love**
	69	**Towpath**
TOP30	70	**Wilton Way Café**

South East London

TOP30	71	**Brown's of Brockley**
	72	**Del'Aziz** Bankside
	73	**The Deptford Project**
	74	**Exchange Coffee**
TOP30	75	**Monmouth Coffee Company** The Borough
TOP30	76	**ScooterCaffè**
	77	**You Don't Bring Me Flowers**

South West London

	78	**Breads Etcetera**
	79	**Brew**
	80	**Daylesford Organic** Pimilco Road
	81	**Di'Zain**
	82	**Federation Coffee**
	83	**Gail's** Battersea
TOP30	84	**The Goodbench**
	85	**Le Pain Quotidien** Parsons Green
	86	**The Roastery** (Bullet Coffee Cartel)

Kensington & Chelsea

	87	**Andronicas World of Coffee** Harrods
	88	**Aubaine** Brompton Cross
	89	**Brompton Quarter Brasserie**
	90	**Caffè Nero** Gloucester Road
	91	**Coffee Plant**
	92	**Garden Café at Buckingham Palace**
	93	**Kensington Square Kitchen**
	94	**Ladurée** Harrods
	95	**Lisboa Patisserie**
	96	**Tom's Deli**
	97	**Tomtom Coffee House**

West London

	98	**Baker & Spice** Maida Vale
	99	**Gail's** Queen's Park
	100	**Indie Coffee**